Banking

Book 1

Virginia Evans
Ken Gilmore, MBA

Express Publishing

Scope and Sequence

Unit	Topic	Reading context	Vocabulary	Function
1	Money	Advertisement	balance, cash, change, check, coin, currency, exchange, exchange rate, fee	Stating total amounts
2	Bank supplies	Email	bill strap, cash, cash drawer, coin, coin wrapper, counterfeit pen, deposit bag, fingerprint pad, ink, pen, stamp	Explaining what you need
3	Bank furniture	Website	armchair, conference table, couch, desk, desk chair, filing cabinet, mat, post, rope, teller pedestal	Making suggestions
4	Bank documents	Teller manual	account application, account statement, balance sheet, cashier's check, change of address, deposit slip, envelope, register, teller receipt, withdrawal form	Requesting identification
5	Bank machines	Website	adding machine, calculator, coin machine, computer, counterfeit detector, currency counter, monitor, printer, security camera, shredder, swipe card reader	Stating requirements
6	Parts of a bank	Bank checklist	breakroom, counter, customer service desk, foyer, lobby, manager's office, safe deposit box, teller station, vault, waiting area	Reporting a problem
7	Numbers	Chart	- hundred, add, and, comes to, divided by, equals, is, less, minus, multiplied by, over, plus, subtract, times	Talking about numbers
8	Savings accounts	Newspaper article	deposit, depositor, earn, interest, interest rate, limit, long-term, minimum balance, savings account, withdrawal	Warning customers
9	Checking accounts	Advertisement	average balance, check, checkbook, checking account, debit, debit card, direct deposit, liquid, maintenance fee, overdraft, returned	Offering a service
10	Credit cards	Business letter	annual fee, approve, APR, balance transfer, cash advance, credit card, credit limit, finance charge, introductory rate	Describing interest rates
11	Access channels	Website	ATM, ATM fee, branch, brick-and-mortar, call center, deposit, drive-up, funds, mobile banking, online banking, PIN, withdraw	Providing options
12	Online banking	Website	bill pay, electronic statement, lock out, log in, paperless, password, phishing, secure, security measures, SSL, transfer	Collecting personal information
13	Office and administrative support	Job postings	accounting clerk, administrative assistant, bookkeeping clerk, branch manager, data entry keyer, greet, head teller, oversee, receptionist, records, support	Describing job duties
14	Phone banker	Letter	answering system, automated, call center, complete, customer service, issue, phone banker, resolve, telephone banking, transaction	Starting a transaction
15	Teller	Job posting	accept, accuracy, calculate, check, count, handle, issue, money order, payment, teller, verify	Talking about job experience

Table of Contents

cash

Welcome to

1 FIRST REGIONAL BANK

Do you need a safe place for your hard-earned **cash**? Open a checking account today!

Are you tired of **coins** and loose **change**? We will count and deposit them for free!

Do you have a paycheck? **Cash** your **check** here, or open an account and make a deposit.

Do you need to **exchange** foreign currency? Here are our **exchange rates***:

CURRENCY	RATE 1 USD	in USD
American Dollar	1 USD	in USD
British Pound	0.616452	1.62219
Euro	0.722857	1.3834
Hong Kong Dollar	7.7903	0.123865
Japanese Yen	81.8708	0.0122144
Mexican Peso	12.097	0.0862251
South Korean Won	1126.1	0.000888
Turkish Lira	1.5991	0.62352

All exchanges are subject to a .09% service **fee**.

Balance your budget at First Regional!

*Rates change hourly

check

coins

Get ready!

❶ Before you read the passage, talk about these questions.

1 What do people use to make purchases in your country?

2 Are coins or bills more common in your country? Which do you prefer?

Reading

❷ Read the bank advertisement. Then, mark the following statements as true (T) or false (F).

1 ___ Customers need an account to cash checks.

2 ___ One Yen is worth less than one USD.

3 ___ The bank exchanges currency for free.

Vocabulary

❸ Match the words (1-5) with the definitions (A-E).

1 ___ fee
2 ___ cash
3 ___ balance
4 ___ coins
5 ___ exchange rate

A the value of a currency in terms of another
B money in the form of metal discs
C an additional cost
D to make accounts even
E money in the form of paper notes and coins

❹ Fill in the blanks with the correct words from the word bank.

word BANK

exchange   change
check   currency   cash

1 He has no bills, just some _____ .

2 _____ your euros before returning from your trip.

3 The vendor did not accept Jon's foreign _____ .

4 The bank refused to _____ his paycheck.

5 Jon wrote a _____ for the gas bill.

5 🎧 Listen and read the bank advertisement again. How many dollars would you need to buy a British pound?

Listening

6 🎧 Listen to a conversation between a customer and a teller. Choose the correct answers.

1 What is the conversation mainly about?
   A opening an account
   B exchanging currency
   C cashing a check
   D depositing money

2 What does the teller warn the man about?
   A a service fee
   B a lack of dollars
   C an incorrect total
   D a low exchange rate

7 🎧 Listen again and complete the conversation.

Teller:	Hello, Sir. Welcome to First Regional Bank. How can I help you?
Tourist:	Hi. I need to **1** _____ these euros for American dollars.
Teller:	All right. Let's see **2** _____ _____ you have there.
Tourist:	Here you go.
Teller:	Twenty, forty, sixty … The **3** _____ comes to one hundred and seventy euros.
Tourist:	How much is that in **4** _____?
Teller:	I'll calculate that now. **5** _____ _____ _____ two hundred and thirty-five dollars and seventeen cents.
Tourist:	Great. Can I make the exchange?
Teller:	Of course. But there is a one percent **6** _____ _____ .

Speaking

8 With a partner, act out the roles below based on Task 7. Then, switch roles.

USE LANGUAGE SUCH AS:

How can I …?
I need to exchange …
The total comes to …

Student A: You are a tourist exchanging currency. Talk to Student B about:
● what currency you have
● what currency you want
● how much money you have

Student B: You are a bank teller. Talk to Student A about exchanging currency.

Writing

9 Use the advertisement and the conversation from Task 8 to fill out the teller's currency exchange form.

1 FIRST REGIONAL BANK
Currency
Exchange Form

Currency presented: _____

Currency requested: _____

Amount presented: _____

Exchange Rate: _____

Amount returned: _____

stamp

coin wrapper

fingerprint pad

Mr. Coleman,

I went through the supplies **inventory** as you asked. Here is a list of the things we need.

> 3 cases of **bill straps**
>
> 6 cases of **coin wrappers**
>
> 1 **cash drawer** with sections for cash and coins (for the new teller station)
>
> 1 **fingerprint pad**
>
> 1 **bottle of ink**
>
> 4 cases of **deposit bags**
>
> 3 date **stamps**
>
> 1 void stamp
>
> 2 boxes of ballpoint **pens**
>
> 6 **counterfeit pens**

That is everything. We are almost out of coin wrappers and deposit bags. We need a shipment by Monday. I will tell you if we get low on anything else.

Thank you,
Sue

Get ready!

❶ Before you read the passage, talk about these questions.

1   What supplies does a bank teller need?

2   What does your bank do when supplies run low?

Reading

❷ Read the email from a teller to a bank manager. Then, choose the correct answers.

1   What is the email mainly about?
   A   items the bank needs
   B   prices of bank supplies
   C   delays of shipments
   D   new teller supplies

2   Which of the following supplies does the bank NOT need?
   A   coin wrappers   C   coins
   B   deposit bags   D   stamps

3   What supplies are nearly gone?
   A   cash drawers   C   teller stations
   B   deposit bags   D   ink pads

Vocabulary

❸ Read the sentence and choose the correct word.

1   Make sure the bill is real with a **counterfeit pen / cash drawer**.

2   He wrapped $500 of cash in a **coin wrapper / bill strap**.

3   Place your thumb on the **fingerprint pad / pen**.

4   Update the **inventory / stamps** with the new supplies.

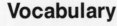
cash drawer

❹ Place the words and phrases from the word bank under the correct heading.

word BANK

ink   stamp   **cash drawer**
pen   coin wrapper   deposit bag

Things to Mark Paper	Containers for Money
_____	_____
_____	_____
_____	_____

❺ 🎧 Listen and read the email again. What is ink contained in?

Listening

❻ 🎧 Listen to a conversation between a bank manager and a teller. Mark the following statements as true (T) or false (F).

1 ___ Old deposit bags are available.

2 ___ The bank has no counterfeit pens.

3 ___ The woman will purchase coin wrappers and bill straps at a store.

❼ 🎧 Listen again and complete the conversation.

Manager:	Hi, Sue. I got your email about the **1** _____ inventory. Thanks for doing that.
Teller:	Oh. No problem. We're pretty **2** _____ _____ those deposit bags.
Manager:	I saw that. If we **3** _____ _____, use the old ones.
Teller:	Got it. We're also **4** _____ _____ counterfeit pens.
Manager:	Well, we can check the **5** _____ by hand until Monday.
Teller:	Okay. **6** _____ _____ the coin wrappers and bill straps?
Manager:	I picked up a box of each at the store. Here you go.
Teller:	Oh, good. Thanks.

Speaking

❽ With a partner, act out the roles below based on Task 7. Then, switch roles.

USE LANGUAGE SUCH AS:

If we run out …

We are also out of …

I picked up …

Student A: You are a bank manager. Talk to Student B about:

● supplies the bank is low on

● supplies the bank is out of

● what to do until supplies arrive

Student B: You are a teller. Talk to Student A about bank supplies.

Writing

❾ Use the email and the conversation from Task 8 to fill out the supplies inventory list.

Bank Supplies Inventory

Quantity	Supplies needed
_____	_____
_____	_____
_____	_____
_____	_____
_____	_____

7

Check out our selection of furniture for banks!

Order online today, or visit a MODERN STYLE location near you!

- We have **filing cabinets** available in seven different colors.
- All **teller pedestals** are currently **20%** off.
- We sell the finest oak and mahogany **desks**. (Each comes with a free desk chair.)
- Our **post** and **rope** sets are classy and practical.
- Peruse our hundreds of choices of **couches** and armchairs.
- Oak laminate **conference tables** are now **30%** off.
- Any order over $900 comes with a free set of carpet floor **mats**.

desk

conference table

desk chair

filing cabinets

Get ready!

❶ Before you read the passage, talk about these questions.

1 What furniture items do you find in a bank?
2 If you were a bank manager, how would you furnish your bank?

Reading

❷ Read the page from a furniture company's website. Then, mark the following statements as true (T) or false (F).

1 ___ Conference tables are on sale.
2 ___ Every desk comes with a free chair.
3 ___ Free mats come with every order.

Vocabulary

❸ Read the sentence pair. Choose where the words best fit the blanks.

1 armchair / teller pedestal
   A Lock the deposit in the _____.
   B The customer sat in the _____.

2 mat / filing cabinet
   A Please wipe your feet on the _____.
   B Mr. Smith put the forms in the _____.

3 rope / conference table
   A The _____ keeps the customer line organized.
   B This _____ seats twelve people.

4 Fill in the blanks with the correct words and phrases from the word bank.

word *BANK*

desks   posts   couch   desk chair

1   A couple is waiting together on the _____ .
2   Connect the _____ with rope.
3   The banker sat down in her _____ .
4   The new _____ have six drawers each.

5 🎧 Listen and read the web page again. What gift is given with large orders?

Listening

6 🎧 Listen to a conversation between a bank manager and an employee. Choose the correct answers.

1   What is the conversation mainly about?
   A   opening a new branch
   B   adding posts and ropes
   C   reorganizing the lobby
   D   replacing old furniture

2   What new furniture will the manager buy?
   A   posts   **C**   armchairs
   B   mats   **D**   ropes

7 🎧 Listen again and complete the conversation.

Manager:	We need to reorganize the lobby.
Employee:	I know what you mean. Customers don't know where the line starts.
Manager:	Let's see. 1 _____ _____ move these armchairs away from the door.
Employee:	Yeah. Then people could walk straight to the 2 _____ .
Manager:	Right. And 3 _____ _____ _____ shift the post and rope setup forward?
Employee:	Then there won't be any confusion about the 4 _____ .
Manager:	Exactly. 5 _____ _____ _____ get some floor mats.
Employee:	6 _____ _____ . Blue ones to match the chairs.

Speaking

8 With a partner, act out the roles below based on Task 7. Then, switch roles.

USE LANGUAGE SUCH AS:

We could move these …
What if we …?
Then there won't be …

Student A: You are a bank manager. Talk to Student B about:
●   an office problem
●   moving furniture
●   purchasing furniture

Student B: You are a bank employee. Talk to Student A about rearranging the bank furniture.

Writing

9 Use the web page and the conversation from Task 8 to fill out the bank employee's after-hours to do list.

To Do ✓

Please rearrange the furniture in the following way.

Move the _____

Shift the _____

Place the new _____

near the _____

9

Get ready!

1 Before you read the passage, talk about these questions.

1 What documents are required to open a bank account in your country?

2 What documents does a teller use in transactions?

FIRST REGIONAL BANK

Teller's Manual

Every morning, be sure to stock the following documents:

✓ **account statement** blanks - These are for customers requesting a copy of their monthly statement.

✓ **account applications** - These are for customers looking to open an account.

✓ **change of address** forms - These are for customers moving to a new address.

✓ **deposit slips** - These are for customers making deposits.

✓ **withdrawal forms** - These are for customers making withdrawals.

✓ **envelopes** - These are for all withdrawals over $100.

✓ **teller receipts** - These are printed after every transaction.

✓ **balance sheet** blanks - These are for customer's requesting to see their balance.

✓ **cashier's checks** - These are recommended as an alternative to cash for large purchases.

✓ customer **registers** - These are for customers wishing to see a detailed account history.

Reading

2 Read the page from a bank teller's manual. Then, choose the correct answers.

1 What is the main purpose of this page?
   A to list items customers need to cash checks
   B to describe papers tellers need for each shift
   C to explain how to open a new account
   D to inform tellers of new transaction guidelines

2 Which of the following documents does NOT show a customer's balance?
   A register   C balance sheet
   B deposit slip   D account statement

3 Which document is for customers who want to receive mail at a different location?
   A withdrawal form   C envelope
   B deposit slip   D change of address

Vocabulary

3 Match the words (1-5) with the definitions (A-E).

1 __ envelope   4 __ account application
2 __ deposit slip   5 __ cashier's check
3 __ register

A a form for opening an account
B a document to use instead of cash
C a detailed history of account transactions
D a paper sleeve to hold a document
E a form to fill out when putting money into an account

deposit slip   envelope   balance sheet   cashier's check

4 Fill in the blanks with the correct words and phrases from the word bank.

 **BANK**

account statement   change of address
teller receipt   withdrawal form   balance sheet

1 Every month, account holders get a(n) _____ .

2 To remove money, fill out a(n) _____ .

3 Provide clients with a(n) _____ after every transaction.

4 A(n) _____ shows a customer's balance.

5 Complete a(n) _____ form before you move.

5 🎧 Listen and read the page again. What is a customer given every time they perform a transaction at a bank?

Listening

6 🎧 Listen to a conversation between a teller and a customer. Mark the following statements as true (T) or false (F).

1 __ The customer asks for a cashier's check.

2 __ The teller gives the customer two documents.

3 __ The customer must have at least $100.

7 🎧 Listen again and complete the conversation.

Teller: 1 _____ , _____ . How can I help you today?

Customer: Hi. I'd like to 2 _____ a checking account.

Teller: Wonderful. Here's an 3 _____ _____ and a pen.

Customer: Okay. Thanks.

Teller: While you are 4 _____ _____ , can I see your driver's license?

Customer: Sure. Here you go.

Teller: Great. Thank you. You'll also have to fill out this 5 _____ _____ .

Customer: Oh. Thanks. Is there a minimum starting 6 _____ ?

Teller: Yes, it's just one hundred dollars.

Speaking

8 With a partner, act out the roles below based on Task 7. Then, switch roles.

USE LANGUAGE SUCH AS:

How can I help you …?

I'd like to …

You'll also have to …

Student A: You are a bank teller. Talk to Student B about:
- an account application
- documents required
- a minimum balance

Student B: You are a bank customer. Talk to Student A about opening a checking account.

Writing

9 Use the page and the conversation from Task 8 to fill out the account application. Make up some personal details for the applicant. Use today's date.

TOWNSMAN'S BANK
Account Application

Type of Account
Checking: ___ Savings: ___

Name: _____

Date: _____

Address: _____

Phone: _____

Starting Balance: _____

Reason for opening account: _____

5 Bank machines

Get ready!

❶ Before you read the passage, talk about these questions.

1 What kinds of machines are used in banks?
2 What security measures do banks take in your country?

security camera

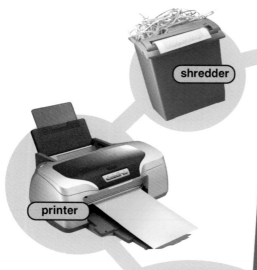

shredder

printer

monitor

adding machine

The Right Place

Buy Banking Necessities
at the Right Place for the Right Price
768-555-2951

Fast coin counters: These machines will also wrap and sort your change.

Currency Counters: Our machines count paper money, coins, or both.

Swipe Card Readers: Our readers are high-quality and easy to use.

Counterfeit Detectors: These detectors are reliable and error-free. You'll never accept false bills again!

Computers: Our computers are programmed especially for bankers. Customers who buy in the next two weeks get a chance to win a FREE monitor.

Printers: Customers will receive 20% off printers with our new computer package.

Adding machines: These **calculators** have a print-out function that your customers will appreciate.

Paper Shredders: Keep your clients' personal information safe. Destroy sensitive documents with our powerful shredders.

Security Cameras: Our high-quality cameras will protect your business.

The Right Place

BANKING NECESSITIES

768-555-2951

Reading

❷ Read the website. Then, mark the following statements as true (T) or false (F).

1 __ The currency counters wrap bills.
2 __ The website is giving away free printers with some computers.
3 __ The adding machines can print answers.

Vocabulary

❸ Match the words (1-5) with the definitions (A-E).

1 __ monitor   4 __ currency counter
2 __ computer   5 __ swipe card reader
3 __ adding machine

A a screen for viewing electronic information
B a device that reads credit or debit cards
C an electronic device that stores information
D a machine that counts paper money or coins
E an electronic device that does math

4 Fill in the blanks with the correct words and phrases from the word bank.

w **ord** **BANK**

printer   calculator   shredder   security camera
coin machine   counterfeit detector

1 Destroy those documents in the _____ .
2 The _____ found fake bills.
3 Police used a _____ to identify the thief.
4 The _____ is out of ink.
5 A _____ makes adding up change much easier.
6 There were many numbers to add, so the worker used a _____ .

5 🎧 Listen and read the website again. What kind of paperwork might a bank wish to dispose of carefully?

Listening

6 🎧 Listen to a conversation between a salesperson and a bank manager. Choose the correct answers.

1 What is the conversation mainly about?
   A a new order   C a broken machine
   B a late shipment   D an order discount

2 What is true of the currency counter?
   A It is slower than the coin counter.
   B It is more expensive than coin counters.
   C It will not work properly when overfilled.
   D It is only capable of counting paper money.

7 🎧 Listen again and complete the conversation.

Salesperson:	Thanks for calling Right Place Supply. How can I help you?
Manager:	Hi, this is Tom Morley with M & P Bank.
Salesperson:	Hello, Mr. Morley. **1** _____ _____ _____ _____ for you today?
Customer:	I want to buy a **2** _____ _____ .
Salesperson:	All right. Do you want a machine that counts **3** _____ _____ or coins?
Customer:	Both. **4** _____ _____ _____ count both.
Salesperson:	Okay. It will be more **5** _____ than a coin counter. Is that all right?
Customer:	That's fine. I'm sure it will save us **6** _____ _____ _____ _____ .

Speaking

8 With a partner, act out the roles below based on Task 7. Then, switch roles.

USE LANGUAGE SUCH AS:
What can I do for you …?
It has to …
It will save …

Student A: You are a bank manager. Talk to Student B about:
● a machine you want
● what it must do
● how it will help

Student B: You are a shop employee. Talk to Student A about their purchase.

Writing

9 Use the website and the conversation from Task 8 to fill out the teller's customer inquiry form.

The Right Place

BANKING NECESSITIES

Name of Caller: _____

Bank where he/she works: _____

Product of Interest: _____

Desired Product Functions: _____
_____

Price: _____

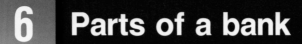

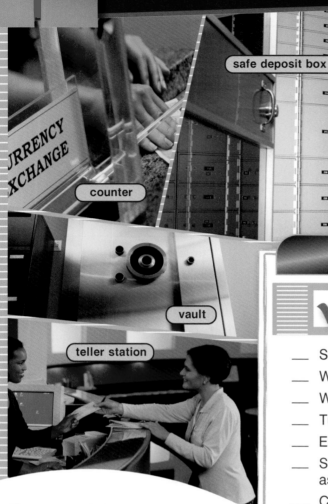

safe deposit box

waiting area

counter

vault

teller station

✓ AM Opening Tasks:

— Sweep the **foyer**. Turn on the main lights.

— Wipe down **counters** in the **lobby**.

— Wipe down counters at the **customer service desk**.

— Turn on the computers at each **teller station**.

— Empty garbage cans in the **waiting area**.

— Start coffee in the **breakroom**. Restock items such as plates, cups, and napkins.

— Check security system of the **safe deposit boxes** and **vault**.

— Turn on lights in the **manager's office**.

— Get cash drawer from the safe in the manager's office.

— Recount and deposit money in your teller station.

Get ready!

❶ **Before you read the passage, talk about these questions.**

1 What are the different parts of a bank?

2 What are some structures that increase security in banks?

Reading

❷ **Read the checklist. Then, fill in the list of rooms and duties.**

Rooms	Duties
Teller Station	1 Turn on _____ . 2 Recount and _____ money.
Foyer	3 _____ .
4 _____	Wipe down counters.
5 _____	Start coffee. Restock supplies.

Vocabulary

❸ **Match the words (1-6) with the definitions (A-F).**

1 __ lobby   4 __ manager's office

2 __ counter   5 __ safe deposit box

3 __ waiting area   6 __ teller station

A a secure metal container

B a space where people wait to be helped

C where bankers process transactions

D a narrow surface

E the place where a supervisor works

F an area at the entrance of a building

4 **Fill in the blanks with the correct words and phrases from the word bank.**

word **BANK**

foyer   vault   breakroom
customer service desk

1 Banks keep most valuables in a
   _____ .

2 The woman entered the bank and stood in the
   _____ .

3 The _____ has tables where
   employees can sit and eat.

4 The young man asked for help at the
   _____ .

5 🎧 **Listen and read the checklist again. What items might you find in a breakroom?**

Listening

6 🎧 **Listen to a conversation between a manager and an employee. Mark the following statements as true (T) or false (F).**

1 __ The employee had trouble with one of the opening tasks.

2 __ The manager tells Ms. Tomlin to call tech services.

3 __ The third teller station will be closed in the morning.

7 🎧 **Listen again and complete the conversation.**

Manager:	How did **1** _____ go this morning, Ms. Tomlin?
Employee:	Everything went pretty well. I **2** _____ _____ starting one of the computers though.
Manager:	Which computer?
Employee:	The one at the third **3** _____ _____ . An error screen came up.
Manager:	I see. We'll have someone **4** _____ _____ _____ at it later.
Employee:	Do you want me to call **5** _____ _____ about it?
Manager:	No, **6** _____ _____ about it. We'll just keep that station closed this morning.

Speaking

8 **With a partner, act out the roles below based on Task 7. Then, switch roles.**

USE LANGUAGE SUCH AS:

How did ...?

Do you want me to ...?

Don't worry about ...

Student A: You are a bank manager. Talk to Student B about:
● the opening tasks
● the problem(s) s/he encountered
● how the problem will be handled

Student B: You are a bank employee. Talk to Student A about opening the bank.

Writing

9 **Use the checklist and the conversation from Task 8 to create an opening checklist.**

CHECKLIST

Foyer: _____

Teller Stations: _____

Breakroom: _____

Manager's Offices: _____

How do they say it?

Symbol	Interpretation	Example	
=	**is, equals, comes to**	½ = 0.5	One-half equals point five.
+	**and, plus, add**	a + b = c	A and B comes to C.
-	**minus, less, subtract**	a – b = c	A less B is C.
x	**times, multiplied by**	a x b = c	A times B equals C.
÷ or /	**over, divided by**	a ÷ b = c or a / b = c	A over B equals C.
1,800	one thousand eight hundred or **eighteen hundred**	The client deposited eighteen hundred dollars.	

Get ready!

❶ Before you read the passage, talk about these questions.

1   How do you say symbols like = and ÷ ?
2   What are some of the ways to say large numbers?

Reading

❷ Read the chart. Then, mark the following statements as true (T) or false (F).

1   __ Six less two means the same thing as six minus two.
2   __ Nine times four equals nine plus four.
3   __ Five over three equals five divided by three.

Vocabulary

❸ Fill in the blanks with the correct words and phrases from the word bank.

word BANK

add	times	less
plus	comes to	hundred

1   Nine _____ two is eighteen.
2   Nine and five _____ fourteen.
3   Thirty _____ six equals twenty-four.
4   One thousand plus two hundred is twelve _____ .
5   To get eight, _____ three and five.
6   Nine _____ two is eleven.

4 **Read the sentence and choose the correct word.**

1 Seven **plus / divided by** three is ten.
2 Nine **over / less** eight equals one.
3 Start with seven, **subtract / add** three: this equals four.
4 Six **multiplied by / divided by** two is twelve.
5 Six **over / plus** three equals two.
6 Twenty **less / divided by** four equals five.
7 Five plus six **equals / over** eleven.

5 🎧 **Listen and read the chart again. What does it mean to say that something 'comes to' something else?**

Listening

6 🎧 **Listen to a conversation between two tellers. Choose the correct answers.**

1 What is the dialogue mostly about?
   A deposit procedures
   B subtracting numbers
   C a mathematical error
   D an incomplete deposit slip

2 What did the man do wrong?
   A He copied a number incorrectly.
   B He subtracted instead of dividing.
   C He multiplied by the wrong number.
   D He wrote down the wrong number of checks.

7 🎧 **Listen again and complete the conversation.**

Teller 1: Karen, can you help me for a second?
Teller 2: Sure, Mike. 1 _____ _____?
Teller 1: Well, something's wrong with this deposit slip. I 2 _____ it all twice, but the total is still wrong.
Teller 2: 3 _____ _____ _____ . There are four checks. Three checks for one hundred dollars. And one for one thousand, three hundred.
Teller 1: Yeah. I multiplied the hundred dollar checks by four and added 4 _____ _____ .
Teller 2: 5 _____ _____ _____ .
Teller 1: What do you mean?
Teller 2: You 6 _____ _____ the wrong number.
Teller 1: Oh, what a simple mistake! Thanks.

Speaking

8 **With a partner, act out the roles below based on Task 7. Then, switch roles.**

USE LANGUAGE SUCH AS:

Can you help me for a second?

Something's wrong with this ...

There are ... checks ...

Student A: You are having trouble with a deposit slip. Ask Student B about:
- your work
- errors
- solutions

Student B: You are a teller. Answer Student A's questions.

Writing

9 **Use the chart and the conversation from Task 8 to fill out the deposit slip correction. Make up some personal details for the account holder.**

Account Holder: _____
Account Number: _____

Original Deposit Amount: _____
New Deposit Amount: _____

Explanation of Change: _____
_____
_____

Manager's Approval: Y / N

DRURY SAVINGS BANK

one-on-one savings plans!

At Drury Savings Bank, our primary goal is customer satisfaction. That's why we encourage you to open a **savings account*** with us. It's a great way to improve your financial stability and quality of life.

Our employees develop one-on-one savings plans. That means each **depositor** receives individual attention from our staff. We're currently offering great **interest rates**. The more you **deposit**, the more **interest** you **earn**. So what are you waiting for? Schedule an appointment, and we'll help plan your **long-term** financial goals.

*All savings accounts have a **minimum balance** requirement. Monthly **withdrawals** are **limited**.

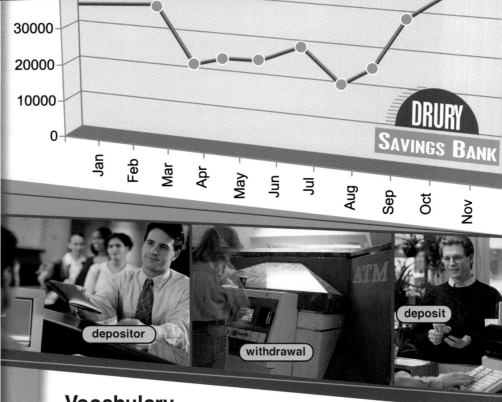

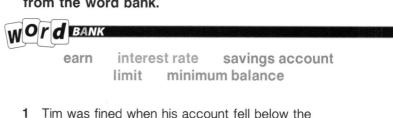

depositor

withdrawal

deposit

Get ready!

1 Before you read the passage, talk about these questions.

1 What encourages people to open savings accounts?

2 What are some restrictions on savings accounts in your country?

Reading

2 Read the bank advertisement. Then, mark the following statements as true (T) or false (F).

1 __ Depositors can develop different savings plans.

2 __ Larger accounts earn more money than smaller accounts.

3 __ Customers can open savings accounts with any amount of money.

Vocabulary

3 Match the words (1-5) with the definitions (A-E).

1 __ deposit   3 __ depositor   5 __ long-term
2 __ interest   4 __ withdrawal

A lasting for a long time
B when you take money from an account
C someone who puts money into an account
D a percentage earned on an amount of money
E to put money into an account

4 Fill in the blanks with the correct words and phrases from the word bank.

word BANK

earn   interest rate   savings account
limit   minimum balance

1 Tim was fined when his account fell below the
_____ .

2 Many banks _____ savings withdrawals to six per year.

3 The woman deposited the money from her paycheck into a(n) _____ .

4 With the high rates, the man was able to _____ some extra money.

5 The man kept his money in an account with an excellent
_____ .

5 🎧 **Listen and read the advertisement again. Is it possible to keep a savings account open with no money in it?**

Listening

6 🎧 **Listen to a conversation between a teller and a customer. Choose the correct answers.**

1 What is the conversation mostly about?
   A making a withdrawal
   B reducing account fees
   C opening a savings account
   D checking on interest rates

2 Why will the man pay a fee?
   A He is opening a new account.
   B He is ordering a cashier's check.
   C He already withdrew money this month.
   D His account doesn't have enough money.

7 🎧 **Listen again and complete the conversation.**

Teller:	Is this correct, Mr. Jones? You want to take three hundred out of your 1 _____ _____?
Customer:	That's right. Why, is there a problem?
Teller:	A small one. You have the money. But your account is 2 _____ to one withdrawal a month.
Customer:	Oh, and I 3 _____ _____ money last week to make a cashier's check. Well, I really need the cash.
Teller:	Are you sure? There will be a 4 _____ .
Customer:	5 _____ _____ is it?
Teller:	It's twenty dollars.
Customer:	I don't 6 _____ _____ _____ . I'll just pay the fee.

DRURY
SAVINGS BANK

Speaking

8 **With a partner, act out the roles below based on Task 7. Then, switch roles.**

Student A: You are a teller. Talk to Student B about:
- his/her account
- the withdrawal limit
- the fee he must pay to withdraw

Student B: You are a customer. Talk to Student A about the withdrawal limit fee.

Writing

9 **Use the advertisement and the conversation from Task 8 to fill out the paperwork.**

Customer Name: _____

Account Number: _____

Type of Transaction: _____

Fee: Y / N

If yes, reason for fee: _____
_____
_____

Fee Amount: _____

Total Transaction Amount: _____

check

checkbook

debit card

VISA

BANK of the NORTHWEST Checking

Are your **liquid** assets protected? Keep your money safe with Bank of the Northwest. We offer two options for **checking accounts**. Which option is right for you?

Basic Checking with no monthly fee	Premium Checking with low monthly maintenance fee
• Deduct funds conveniently with your **checkbook** or **debit card**. • Participating employers can pay you with **direct deposit**. • Pay fees only if you have **overdrafts** or **checks** that are **returned**.	• Premium Checking includes everything that comes with Basic Checking. • Earn interest by maintaining a minimum **average balance**. • The Overdraft Protection Plan prevents fees if you accidentally **debit** too much.

Get ready!

1 Before you read the passage, talk about these questions.

1 What are the advantages of storing money in a bank?

2 What are some different ways that people can pay for purchases?

Reading

2 Read the brochure. Then, mark the following statements as true (T) or false (F).

1 __ Basic Checking carries fees for returned checks.

2 __ Both services allow the use of debit cards.

3 __ Premium Checking does not include direct deposit.

Vocabulary

3 Read the sentence and choose the correct word or phrase.

1 Paul got paid weekly by **average balance / direct deposit**.

2 Olivia paid with cash because she lost her **checkbook / checking account**.

3 The bank charges extra fees for **returned / liquid** checks.

4 Eddie wrote a **check / debit** for his new car.

5 The bank issues **overdrafts / debit cards** with all accounts.

4 Fill in the blanks with the correct words and phrases: *debited, maintenance fee, liquid, average balance, checking account, overdraft*.

1 The bank accidentally _____ a customer's account for duplicate transactions.

2 The annual fees are based on an account's _____ over the year.

3 A(n) _____ is a safe place to store your money.

4 Tom switched to a new bank that does not charge a(n) _____ .

5 Julian will have a(n) _____ if he spends any more money this week.

6 Phoebe's business makes a lot of money, but none of it is _____ .

debit

5 🎧 Listen and read the brochure again. How can a customer take money out of their account?

Listening

6 🎧 Listen to a conversation between a bank agent and a customer. Choose the correct answers.

1 Why is the customer at the bank?
   A to get details about Premium Checking
   B to open her first checking account
   C to learn about checking account options
   D to find a service without overdraft fees

2 What can you infer about Basic Checking?
   A It requires extra paperwork.
   B It includes fees for overdrafts.
   C It is the most popular checking option.
   D It has more benefits than Premium checking.

7 🎧 Listen again and complete the conversation.

Agent:	What **1** _____ _____ _____ for you today, ma'am?
Customer:	I'm thinking about opening a **2** _____ _____ for my son.
Agent:	Well, you came to **3** _____ _____ _____ . Can I interest you in our Premium Checking?
Customer:	What does that include?
Agent:	For a low monthly fee, you get protection against **4** _____ _____ .
Customer:	I don't think he needs that. **5** _____ _____ _____ anything without a fee?
Agent:	Certainly. Our Basic Checking is available at no cost. Of course, there's no overdraft protection either. **6** _____ _____ _____ and we'll get started with the paperwork.

Speaking

8 With a partner, act out the roles below based on Task 7. Then, switch roles.

USE LANGUAGE SUCH AS:

I'm thinking about …

Can I interest you …?

Our Basic Checking …

Student A: You are a bank agent. Talk to Student B about:
● checking accounts
● available features

Student B: You are a bank customer. Talk to Student A about checking account options.

Writing

9 Use the brochure and the conversation from Task 8 to fill out the application for a checking account. Make up a name for the customer.

BANK of the NORTHWEST

Checking Account Application

Name: _____

Account type? Basic / Premium

List any additional services you are looking for in a checking account: _____

_____

_____

_____

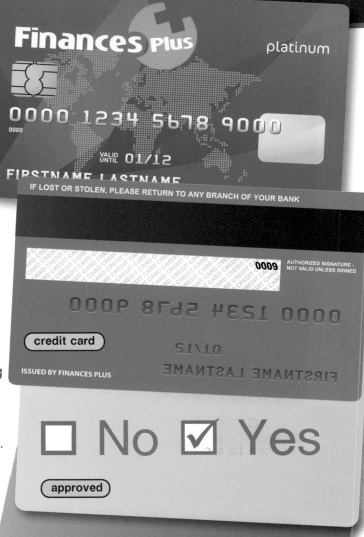

Get ready!

❶ Before you read the passage, talk about these questions.

1 Why do people use credit cards instead of cash?

2 What are some risks of using credit cards?

Dear Mr. Perez,

Congratulations! Finances Plus has **approved** your credit application. You may begin using your new **credit card** right away. Please review the following details about your account.

Credit: Your initial **credit limit** is $1500.00. This limit includes the option for **cash advance**. Your limit can increase if you maintain regular payments. You can pay by check or electronic transfer.

Finance charges: There is no **annual fee** for your account. During the first year, you will enjoy the **introductory rate** of 0%*. The account will accrue 12% **APR** after the first year.

Please call with any questions.
Sincerely,
Fiona Martin
Accounts Manager, Finances Plus

*Any **balance transfers** will accrue 1% interest.

Reading

❷ Read the letter and the summary. Then, fill in the blanks with the correct words and phrases from the word bank.

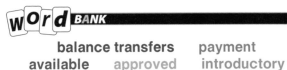

balance transfers	**payment**
available	approved introductory

Mr. Perez's application for a line of credit was **1**_____. Cash advance is **2**_____ towards his credit limit of $1500.00. **3**_____ methods include check and electronic transfer. The account begins with a(n) **4**_____ rate of 0%. The interest rate goes up to 12% after one year. But **5**_____ accrue interest at 1%.

Vocabulary

❸ Match the words (1-6) with the definitions (A-F).

1 _ approve   4 _ finance charge
2 _ annual fee   5 _ balance transfer
3 _ credit limit   6 _ introductory rate

A a low, temporary interest rate
B a cardholder's maximum charge amount
C fees or interest on a credit card account
D to allow or accept something
E a yearly charge for having a credit card
F moving money from one account to another

22

4 Check (✓) the sentence that uses the underlined part correctly.

1 ___ **A** Sharon earned a lower <u>credit limit</u> by paying her bills on time.

 ___ **B** Edwin was upset when his <u>APR</u> increased without notice.

2 ___ **A** One of Raymond's <u>finance charges</u> was the car he bought with his credit card.

 ___ **B** Thelma needs a <u>cash advance</u> to make a purchase.

3 ___ **A** The company has no money because the bank <u>approved</u> its loan.

 ___ **B** The clothing company requires a <u>credit card</u> for all online purchases.

5 🎧 Listen and read the letter again. What transaction would Mr. Perez have to pay for in the year he opened his account?

Listening

6 🎧 Listen to a conversation between a credit card company representative and a customer. Mark the following statements as true (T) or false (F).

1 ___ The customer wants a new line of credit.

2 ___ The man's interest rate is now 12%.

3 ___ The man's interest rate will increase.

7 🎧 Listen again and complete the conversation.

Representative:	Finances Plus, Carol speaking. How can I help you?
Customer:	Hi, I just got a card and I'm confused about my 1 _____ _____ .
Representative:	What 2 _____ _____ _____ the problem?
Customer:	Well, I thought the interest 3 _____ _____ zero. This letter says it's twelve percent.
Representative:	Okay, I can 4 _____ _____ . Your introductory rate is zero percent.
Customer:	Oh, wonderful.
Representative:	But next November, your rate 5 _____ _____ to twelve percent.
Customer:	Oh, 6 _____ _____ _____ . Thanks for your help.

Speaking

8 With a partner, act out the roles below based on Task 7. Then, switch roles.

USE LANGUAGE SUCH AS:

How can I ...?

I'm confused ...

Thanks for your help ...

Student A: You are a credit card company representative. Talk to Student B about:
- his/her account
- introductory interest rates
- interest rate changes

Student B: You are a credit card customer. Talk to Student A about your interest rates.

Writing

9 Use the letter and the conversation from Task 8 to fill out the approval form.

Finances Plus

APPROVAL FOR LINE OF CREDIT

Customer name: _____

Introductory rate: _____

Credit limit: _____

Other fees and restrictions: _____
_____

FERDINAND'S BANK

drive-up

mobile banking

online banking

ATM

Access

Why bank with Ferdinand's?
We offer the most benefits.

Convenient **branches**

Ferdinand's has **brick-and-mortar** facilities in nearly every city. Our **drive-up** windows make banking fast and easy. Make a quick **deposit** and get on your way.

International **ATMs**

Do you need to **withdraw** money while traveling? You will find Ferdinand's ATMs around the world, free of charge. Why pay costly **ATM fees** with other banks? Just bring your debit card and **PIN**.

24-hour support

Talk to a specialist in our 24-hour **call center**. Call to check your available **funds** or locate the nearest ATM.

Banking anywhere

Access your account from home with **online banking**. Or use your cell phone for **mobile banking**.

Get ready!

❶ Before you read the passage, talk about these questions.

1 How do bank customers access their money?

2 What are the easiest ways to access a bank account in your country?

Reading

❷ Read the website. Then, mark the following statements as true (T) or false (F).

1 __ Drive-up windows are available at brick-and-mortar facilities.

2 __ The bank has brick and mortar facilities around the world.

3 __ Customers can speak to bank representatives any time of day.

Vocabulary

❸ Read the sentence pair. Choose where the words best fit the blanks.

1 **call center / ATM**

A Rachel's job at the _____ involves answering questions from customers.

B Kevin dislikes going inside the bank so he uses the _____ .

2 **online banking / mobile banking**

A Yuri uses _____ to check her bank balance from her work computer.

B Smart phones allow _____ to occur, even while customers ride the bus.

3 **deposit / ATM fee**

A Many banks charge a(n) _____ if you use a debit card from another bank.

B Pierre had an overdraft because he forgot to make a(n) _____ .

4 **Fill in the blanks with the correct words and phrases:**
funds, drive-up, withdraw, brick-and-mortar, PIN, branch.

1 Robert pulled his car up to the _____ window.

2 Lisa could not use the ATM because she forgot her
_____ .

3 Boris prefers _____ facilities to online banking
because he can talk to a person.

4 The Bank of Oakville opened a new _____ on
D Street.

5 Your _____ are not available until the day after
you make a deposit.

6 Nancy tried to _____ more money than she had,
but the manager refused to allow it.

5 🎧 **Listen and read the website again. Where does
Ferdinand's Bank have ATMs located?**

Listening

6 🎧 **Listen to a conversation between a bank customer
and a teller. Choose the correct answers.**

1 Why is the customer upset?

A He cannot find his debit card.

B He could not access the ATM.

C He was unable to make a deposit.

D He could not find a bank while traveling.

2 What can you infer about ATM deposits?

A They do not always require a PIN.

B They are not available immediately.

C They cannot be made in other countries.

D They are less secure than branch deposits.

7 🎧 **Listen again and complete the conversation.**

Customer:	Finally! I tried to make this deposit twice this week, but **1** _____ _____ _____ .
Teller:	I'm so sorry for the inconvenience, sir. Maybe I can help. Do you have a **2** _____ _____?
Customer:	I do. But I leave it at home, just to be safe.
Teller:	Well, we offer a 24-hour ATM to make deposits. It's right outside. The transaction goes through on the **3** _____ _____ _____ .
Customer:	**4** _____ _____ . But I travel a lot.
Teller:	Just call our **5** _____ _____ . They'll direct you to the closest ATM.
Customer:	Okay. I'll try that **6** _____ _____ .

Speaking

8 **With a partner, act out the
roles below based on Task 7.
Then, switch roles.**

USE LANGUAGE SUCH AS:

I tried to … but …

Sorry for the inconvenience.

Call our …

Student A: You are a bank
customer. Talk to Student B
about:

● an inconvenience

● making a deposit

Student B: You are a bank
customer. Talk to Student A
about making deposits.

Writing

9 **Use the website and the
conversation from Task 8 to
fill out the customer's notes.**

FERDINAND'S BANK

**Customer's
NOTES**

The different ways to make deposits
are …

_____

To use an ATM, I need …

_____

When traveling, I can find an ATM by …

_____

_____

25

12 Online banking

Get ready!

❶ Before you read the passage, talk about these questions.

1 What are the benefits of online banking?

2 What are the risks of online banking?

Forestwood Bank_Online Banking

At Forestwood Bank, we employ a variety of **security measures** to keep our customers' information safe. All our customers' accounts are **password** protected. Our computer system **locks out** users after failed **log in** attempts. Accounts are unlocked only when you confirm details over the phone or in person.

Once you log in, your information is even more secure. Our **SSL** encryption protects every **bill pay** transaction, **transfer**, and loan application. With Forestwood Bank, your money is safe online.

But customers should protect themselves, too. Know the difference between our **paperless electronic statements** and **phishing** attempts. Forestwood will NEVER ask for sensitive information in an email.

Reading

❷ Read the web page from Forestwood Bank. Then, choose the correct answers.

1 What is the purpose of the web page?

A to discuss the safety of online banking

B to describe the dangers of phishing attempts

C to show how to receive paperless statements

D to explain the need for new security measures

2 All of the following are features of online banking except

A bill pay.   C account unlocking.

B loan application.   D electronic statements.

3 What can you infer about phishing attempts?

A They use SSL encryption.

B They request sensitive information.

C They occur during bill pay transactions.

D They are prevented by locking out customers.

Vocabulary

❸ Match the words (1-5) with the definitions (A-E).

1 __ bill pay

2 __ paperless

3 __ secure

4 __ password

5 __ transfer

A to move funds from one account to another

B a service that sends money to businesses from bank accounts

C being safe

D a code that provides access to an account

E not using paper

4 Fill in the blanks with the correct words and phrases from the word bank.

Word BANK

electronic statements   security measures
SSL   **phishing**   lock out   log in

1 A thief accessed the account through a(n) _____ scam.

2 The bank sends _____ monthly.

3 A(n) _____ connection keeps online information hidden.

4 To _____, enter your password.

5 This system will _____ customers after three incorrect passwords are entered.

6 Most banks offer several _____ to keep account information safe.

5 🎧 Listen and read the web page again. What should the bank's customers not give out in response to an email?

Listening

6 🎧 Listen to a conversation between a bank employee and a customer. Mark the following statements as true (T) or false (F).

1 __ The man calls about a phishing attempt.

2 __ The man asks for a new password.

3 __ The woman unlocks the man's account.

7 🎧 Listen again and complete the conversation.

Teller:	Forestwood Bank, Shirley speaking. How may I help you?
Caller:	Hi I'm **1** _____ _____ of my online account. I typed my password wrong a few times.
Teller:	Okay, I can unlock that. **2** _____ _____ _____ your name and date of birth.
Caller:	My name is Richard Hanson. I was born January 10th, 1973.
Teller:	**3** _____ _____ last four digits of your account?
Caller:	**4** _____ _____ . It's 8932.
Teller:	Thank you, Mr. Hanson. Now, what is your **5** _____?
Caller:	It's Hanson one two two. All one word.
Teller:	Okay. Your account is **6** _____ .

Speaking

8 With a partner, act out the roles below based on Task 7. Then, switch roles.

USE LANGUAGE SUCH AS:

How may I help you?

I typed …

What is your … ?

Student A: You are a bank employee. Talk to Student B about:
● an account lock out
● account information
● password

Student B: You are a customer. Talk to Student A about unlocking it.

Writing

9 Use the web page and the conversation from Task 8 to fill out the call record.

Call 19841

Customer: _____

Date of Birth: _____

Account: _____

Password: _____

Reason for call: _____

Was customer's problem resolved? If yes, how? _____

_____

_____

greet

FIRST CITIZENS BANK
Job Listings

First Citizens Bank is now hiring the following positions. Include resume, cover letter, and references with application.

Receptionist
Duties: **greeting** visitors, answering phones, and directing customers.

Administrative Assistant
Duties: **supporting** branch manager by organizing schedules, paperwork, and mail.

Head teller
Position requires two years' experience. Duties: creating schedules, managing cash drawers and reviewing teller transaction records.

Entry Keyer
Typing proficiency is required, but experience is not. Duties: entering **records** and data. Keyers report to both the **accounting clerk** and **bookkeeping clerk**.

Branch Manager
The branch manager **oversees** and administers all tasks. Duties include: building a strong relationship with the community, interviewing applicants, approving loans and assisting customers.

branch manager

entry keyer

Get ready!

❶ Before you read the passage, talk about these questions.

1 What are some jobs people have in banks?

2 Which bank jobs are the most difficult? Why?

Reading

❷ Read the job listings for a nationwide bank. Then, mark the following statements as true (T) or false (F).

1 __ All of the positions require references.

2 __ Head teller applicants must be skilled typists.

3 __ Branch managers interview potential employees.

Vocabulary

❸ Read the sentence pair. Choose where the words best fit the blanks.

1 **receptionist / bookkeeping clerk**

  A A _____ updates financial records.

  B The _____ answers phones and greets customers.

2 **entry keyer / head teller**

  A The _____ must schedule the tellers' shifts.

  B A(n) _____ works on a computer all day.

3 **support / greet**

  A _____ all customers with a smile.

  B The assistant's job is to _____ the branch manager.

4 Match the words (1-5) with the definitions (A-E).

1 ___ oversee
2 ___ records
3 ___ administrative assistant
4 ___ branch manager
5 ___ accounting clerk

A an employee that tracks financial records
B an employee that runs an entire bank branch
C an employee that helps with various office tasks
D to supervise
E documents

5 🎧 Listen and read the job listings again. Which positions involve dealing directly with the bank's customers?

Listening

6 🎧 Listen to a conversation between a branch manager and a new employee. Check (✓) the positions the manager describes.

1 ❑ branch manager
2 ❑ administrative assistant
3 ❑ head teller
4 ❑ bookkeeping clerk
5 ❑ receptionist

7 🎧 Listen again and complete the conversation.

Manager:	Welcome to your first day on the job. I'll 1 _____ _____ _____ .
Employee:	Great, thanks.
Manager:	This is the 2 _____ _____ office. Bring all of your paperwork here at the end of the day.
Employee:	Like my balance sheet?
Manager:	Precisely. Now, this is Mr. Dahl's office. He's the 3 _____ _____ . So if you ever have a problem, see him first.
Employee:	4 _____ _____ .
Manager:	Finally, this is my 5 _____ _____ desk. She can answer just about any question you have.
Employee:	I see. I 6 _____ _____ to get started.

Speaking

8 With a partner, act out the roles below based on Task 7. Then, switch roles.

USE LANGUAGE SUCH AS:

Welcome to your first day …

This is the … office.

If you ever have a problem …

Student A: You are a branch manager. Talk to Student B about:
● bank offices
● other positions
● other position responsibilities

Student B: You are a new employee. Talk to Student A about other positions at the bank.

Writing

9 Use the job listings and the conversation from Task 8 to fill out the job descriptions.

Job Title: _____

Responsibilities: _____

_____

Job Title: _____

Responsibilities: _____

_____

Job Title: _____

Responsibilities: _____

_____

Get ready!

1 **Before you read the passage, talk about these questions.**

1 What are some reasons for people choosing telephone banking?

2 What are the benefits of making transactions by telephone?

February 9

Jack Niles, Manager
Kopps Savings Bank
485 Elm Street, Jefferson, IL

Kopps Savings Bank

Dear Valued Account Holder,

We would like to tell you about our new **telephone banking system**. This is not just another **automated answering system**. This is an opportunity for us to offer you great **customer service**!

Starting March 1, you will have access to our **call center**. **Phone bankers** will be available during normal business' hours. You'll be able to **complete** all **transactions** by phone if you choose. Our phone bankers have the same capabilities as any other banker. Call to **resolve issues** with your account or to make money transfers.

We hope that you enjoy our new telephone banking system.

Sincerely,
Jack Niles

call center

Reading

2 **Read the letter. Then, choose the correct answers.**

1 What is this letter mostly about?

   A how to become a telephone banker

   B the benefits of telephone banking

   C how to make transactions via telephone

   D issues with automated answering systems

2 Which is NOT included in the letter?

   A the capabilities of phone tellers

   B the hours that the service will be available

   C the price of the telephone banking service

   D a starting date for the telephone banking system

3 What is one benefit of phone banking?

   A It is faster because it is automated.

   B It helps bank customers save money.

   C All transactions can be made by phone.

   D Customers can reach tellers after business' hours.

Vocabulary

3 **Match the words (1-4) with the definitions (A-D).**

1 __ issue   3 __ transaction

2 __ automated   4 __ customer service

A an exchange of money

B operating without human involvement

C meeting the needs of customers

D a problem or complaint

4 Fill in the blanks with the correct words and phrases from the word bank.

wOrd BANK

resolve   complete   telephone banking
call center   phone banker   answering systems

1 The banker needed an account number to _____ the transaction.

2 A client scheduled a meeting to _____ the problem.

3 _____ allows people to bank from any location with a phone.

4 Two hundred people work at the _____ .

5 A _____ has the same duties as any other banker.

6 Many _____ are automated and need no human operator.

5 🎧 Listen and read the letter again. When will the new service begin?

Listening

6 🎧 Listen to a conversation between a phone banker and a customer. Mark the following statements as true (T) or false (F).

1 __ The man wants to make a withdrawal.

2 __ The woman asks for the man's password.

3 __ The man must visit the bank to complete the transaction.

7 🎧 Listen again and complete the conversation.

Banker:	Kopps Savings Bank. **1** _____ _____ _____ help you?
Customer:	I'm calling to make a **2** _____ .
Banker:	Okay. Your name and **3** _____ _____ number please?
Customer:	Chris Riley. 285 023 5519.
Banker:	Thank you, Mr. Riley. What kind of **4** _____ would you like to make today?
Customer:	I want to move $400 from my **5** _____ _____ into savings.
Banker:	We can do **6** _____ .

Speaking

8 With a partner, act out the roles below based on Task 7. Then, switch roles.

USE LANGUAGE SUCH AS:

How may I ...?

What kind of transaction ...?

We can ...

Student A: You are a telephone banker. Talk to Student B about:
- the transaction
- identification
- what is required

Student B: You are calling a phone banker. Talk to Student A about the transaction you want to make.

Writing

9 Use the letter and the conversation from Task 8 to update the banking file.

Phone Teller: _____

Customer Name: _____

Account Number: _____

Desired Service: _____

_____

_____

Get ready!

❶ Before you read the passage, talk about these questions.

1 What are the responsibilities of tellers?

2 What skills are tellers required to have?

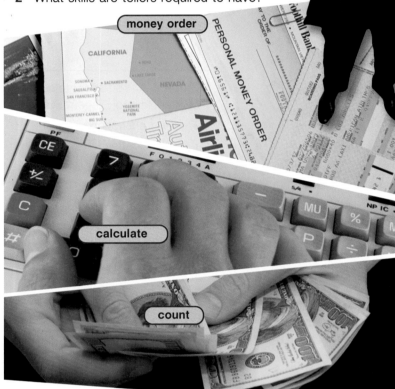

money order

calculate

count

Now hiring

Teller needed at Max & Jones Associated Bank. Applicant must be comfortable **handling** money and mentally **calculating** sums. High school diploma and two years' experience in position required.
Job Responsibilities:
- **Count** cash at the beginning of each shift.
- Identify customers and **check** the **accuracy** of their withdrawal and deposit slips.
- Record all transactions efficiently.
- **Issue** traveler's checks and **money orders**.
- **Accept** and **verify** loan and mortgage payments.
- Answer questions and resolve problems our customers have with their accounts. Do not attempt to answer a question if you are unsure - refer the customer to a manager.
- Promote our banking services.
- Balance cash at the end of each shift.
If you believe you meet these requirements, please stop in for an application.
Max & Jones Bank, 428 Park Drive

Reading

❷ Read the job posting. Then, choose the correct answers.

1 What is the main purpose of this ad?

  A to recruit applicants for a position

  B to help people become better tellers

  C to outline bank operating procedures

  D to promote the banking services at Max & Jones

2 Which of the following is NOT required of the applicants?

  A a college degree

  B mental math skills

  C ability to count efficiently

  D prior experience issuing money orders

3 What can you infer about the people who are hired?

  A They are college-graduates.

  B They hold accounts at the bank.

  C They have previous experience as tellers.

  D They are better at math than communicating.

Vocabulary

❸ Match the words (1-6) with the definitions (A-F).

1 __ issue   4 __ count

2 __ handle   5 __ payment

3 __ check   6 __ money order

A to add up

B a written request for money to be given

C to work with

D money given or received

E to inspect

F to give something

4 Fill in the blanks with the correct words from the word bank.

word BANK

calculate   verified   teller   accuracy   accept

1 Tellers must _____ large sums mentally.
2 She could not _____ the check because it wasn't signed.
3 The banker _____ that she had given the customer the correct amount.
4 Someone who handles transactions at a bank is a _____ .
5 _____ is important in all matters that concern money.

5 🎧 Listen and read the job posting again. How can someone apply for the position advertised?

Listening

6 🎧 Listen to a conversation between an interviewer and an applicant. Mark the following statements as true (T) or false (F).

1 __ The woman has experience as a teller.
2 __ The woman issued mortgage loans.
3 __ The woman was a math tutor in college.

7 🎧 Listen again and complete the conversation.

Interviewer:	Are you ready to begin the interview, Ms. Nelson?
Applicant:	I am. Thanks for seeing me.
Interviewer:	First, I want to know about your 1 _____ _____ . It says on your application you have experience handling money.
Applicant:	That's right. I was a teller for 2 _____ _____ .
Interviewer:	All right. And what were your job 3 _____?
Applicant:	I issued money orders and 4 _____ mortage payment transactions.
Interviewer:	Great. How are your 5 _____ _____?
Applicant:	I'd say they're very good, sir. I took two 6 _____ _____ math classes in college.

Speaking

8 With a partner, act out the roles below based on Task 7. Then, switch roles.

USE LANGUAGE SUCH AS:

I want to know about …
It says on your application …
How are your …?

Student A: You are an interviewer. Talk to Student B about:
● prior experience
● skills

Student B: You are being interviewed. Talk to Student A about your qualifications.

Writing

9 Use the job posting and the conversation from Task 8 to make notes on an interview.

Applicant Name: _____

Prior Experience: _____
_____

Skills: _____
_____
_____

Glossary

accept [V-T-U15] To **accept** is to agree to take something.

account application [N-COUNT-U4] An **account application** is a form someone fills out to open an account at a bank.

account statement [N-COUNT-U4] An **account statement** is a document sent periodically to the customer of a bank showing an account's balance and recent activity.

accounting clerk [N-COUNT-U13] An **accounting clerk** is an employee who monitors financial transactions for an institution.

accuracy [N-UNCOUNT-U15] **Accuracy** is the state of being correct.

add [V-T-U7] To **add** numbers is to combine them.

adding machine [N-COUNT-U5] An **adding machine** is an electronic device that does math.

administrative assistant [N-COUNT-U13] An **administrative assistant** is an employee that performs a variety of administrative tasks in an office.

and [CONJ-U7] **And** is used when combining or adding numbers. For example, one and one equals two.

annual fee [N-COUNT-U10] An **annual fee** is a charge that a credit card holder pays yearly to maintain use of the credit card.

answering system [N-COUNT-U14] An **answering system** is a telephone service where a machine responds to the needs of the caller.

approve [V-T-U10] To **approve** something is to officially allow or accept it.

APR [N-UNCOUNT-U10] **APR**, or annual percentage rate, is the interest rate that a credit card holder pays over one year.

armchair [N-COUNT-U3] An **armchair** is a soft piece of furniture on which one person can sit comfortably.

ATM [N-COUNT-U11] An **ATM**, or automatic teller machine, is a machine that people use to remove money from bank accounts by using a debit card.

ATM fee [N-COUNT-U11] An **ATM fee** is a charge for using a particular bank's ATM.

automated [ADJ-U14] If a system is **automated** it performs mechanically and without human involvement.

average balance [N-COUNT-U9] An **average balance** is an average amount of money that exists in a bank account over time. It is usually used to calculate interest and fees on the account.

balance [V-T-U1] To **balance** amounts of money is to adjust accounts so that all funds are in appropriate places.

balance sheet [N-COUNT-U4] A **balance sheet** is a document that shows an analysis of a bank customer's assets and liabilities.

balance transfer [N-COUNT-U10] A **balance transfer** is the process of moving money from one financial account into another.

bill pay [N-UNCOUNT-U12] **Bill pay** is a service banks offer that allows customers to pay bills by transferring money directly from their accounts to businesses.

bill strap [N-COUNT-U2] A **bill strap** is a strip of printed paper used to wrap specified amounts of cash.

bookkeeping clerk [N-COUNT-U13] A **bookkeeping clerk** is an employee who updates and maintains the financial records of an institution.

branch [N-COUNT-U11] A **branch** is one of a bank's local offices.

branch manager [N-COUNT-U13] A **branch manager** is an employee who is responsible for the operation of a branch of an institution.

breakroom [N-COUNT-U6] A **breakroom** is a space designated for relaxing at work.

brick-and-mortar [ADJ-U11] If a business is **brick-and-mortar**, it has physical stores or offices, rather than existing exclusively online.

calculate [V-T-U15] To **calculate** an answer is to determine it using math.

calculator [N-COUNT-U5] A **calculator** is a handheld electronic device that does math.

call center [N-COUNT-U11] A **call center** is an office where employees of a particular company take phone calls from their customers.

call center [N-COUNT-U14] A **call center** is a place where operators receive phone calls and provide assistance to callers.

cash [N-UNCOUNT-U1] **Cash** is money in the form of government printed, paper bank notes and coins that can be used to make purchases.

cash [V-T-U1] To **cash** a check is to bring it to a bank and exchange it for money in the form of cash.

cash advance [N-COUNT-U10] A **cash advance** is a service provided by a credit card company that allows the user to withdraw an amount in cash within the user's credit limit.

cash drawer [N-COUNT-U2] A **cash drawer** is a sliding compartment with several sections for organizing various denominations of cash and coins.

cashier's check [N-COUNT-U4] A **cashier's check** is a check that is guaranteed by a bank for a specific amount of money.

change [N-UNCOUNT-U1] **Change** is a small amount of money made up of coins, or an amount of money returned to a purchaser who presented more money for payment than was due.

change of address form [N-COUNT-U4] A **change of address form** is a form someone fills out to notify the bank that s/he is to receive mail at a different location.

check [N-COUNT-U9] A **check** is a piece of paper that is used to transfer money from one person's checking account to another person.

check [V-T-U15] To **check** something is to inspect it.

checkbook [N-COUNT-U9] A **checkbook** is a book of checks for removing money from a particular checking account.

checking account [N-COUNT-U9] A **checking account** is an account that someone holds at a bank that allows the holder to write checks or use a debit card to remove money.

coin [N-COUNT-U1] A **coin** is money in the form of a small disc of imprinted metal.

coin machine [N-COUNT-U5] A **coin machine** is a machine that counts coins.

coin wrapper [N-COUNT-U2] A **coin wrapper** is a strip of printed paper used to wrap specified amounts of coins.

come to [V-PHRASE-U7] To **come to** a number is to equal that number.

complete [V-I or T-U14] To **complete** is to finish a process.

computer [N-COUNT-U5] A **computer** is an electronic device that stores and processes information.

conference table [N-COUNT-U3] A **conference table** is a long table around which people sit during a meeting.

couch [N-COUNT-U3] A **couch** is a large soft piece of furniture on which two or more people can sit comfortably.

count [V-I or T-U15] To **count** is to add items to determine a total.

counter [N-COUNT-U6] A **counter** is a narrow table.

counterfeit detector [N-COUNT-U5] A **counterfeit detector** is a device that detects fake money.

counterfeit pen [N-COUNT-U2] A **counterfeit pen** identifies inauthentic paper money.

Glossary

credit card [N-COUNT-U10] A **credit card** is a small, plastic card that is used to pay for something with money that the user will give to the credit card company later.

credit limit [N-COUNT-U10] A **credit limit** is an amount of money that a bank or credit card company allows a user to spend before the borrowed money must be paid back.

currency [N-UNCOUNT-U1] **Currency** is anything used as a medium of exchange, or money in its various forms.

currency counter [N-COUNT-U5] A **currency counter** is a machine that counts paper money or coins.

customer service [N-UNCOUNT-U14] **Customer service** is the act of a company meeting the needs of its customers.

customer service desk [N-COUNT-U6] A **customer service desk** is an area designated to addressing the questions and complaints of customers.

debit [V-T-U9] To **debit** an amount is to remove it from a bank account.

debit card [N-COUNT-U9] A **debit card** is a small, plastic card that is used to remove money from a checking account for a payment. A debit card removes money electronically through a machine at the point of purchase.

deposit [N-COUNT-U11] A **deposit** is an amount of money that someone puts into a bank account in one transaction.

deposit [V-T-U8] To **deposit** is to put money into the bank.

deposit bag [N-COUNT-U2] A **deposit bag** holds money that is to be deposited into a bank account.

deposit slip [N-COUNT-U4] A **deposit slip** is a small sheet of paper someone fills out when he or she puts money into a bank account.

depositor [N-COUNT-U8] A **depositor** puts money into a bank account.

desk [N-COUNT-U3] A **desk** is a piece of furniture with a writing surface and drawers at which a person sits to complete paperwork or other tasks.

desk chair [N-COUNT-U3] A **desk chair** is a piece of furniture with a seat, a back, and sometimes wheels, on which a person sits at a desk.

direct deposit [N-UNCOUNT-U9] **Direct deposit** is the process of putting money into someone else's bank account electronically, without using cash or checks.

divided by [V-PHRASE-U7] If a number is **divided by** another, it is split into that number.

drive-up [ADJ-U11] If something is **drive-up**, it is used by someone who remains in his or her car during the transaction.

earn [V-T-U8] To **earn** is to make a profit.

electronic statement [N-COUNT-U12] An **electronic statement** is a bank document showing account information that is delivered by email.

entry keyer [N-COUNT-U13] An **entry keyer** is an employee who enters data into a computer.

envelope [N-COUNT-U4] An **envelope** is a paper sleeve for containing and transporting money or paper documents.

equal [V-T-U7] To **equal** a number is to be the correct answer to a mathematical problem.

exchange [V-T-U1] To **exchange** something is to give it to someone and receive something else in return.

exchange rate [N-COUNT-U1] An **exchange rate** is the specified worth of one currency in terms of another.

fee [N-COUNT-U1] A **fee** is an amount of money charged to complete a particular action.

filing cabinet [N-COUNT-U3] A **filing cabinet** is a rectangular box with drawers for organizing paper documents in file folders.

finance charge [N-COUNT-U10] A **finance charge** is the overall cost of having a credit card, including charges from interest and fees.

fingerprint pad [N-COUNT-U2] A **fingerprint pad** is a small section of foam-like material for administering ink to make a fingerprint.

foyer [N-COUNT-U6] A **foyer** is an area at the entrance of a building.

funds [N-UNCOUNT-U11] **Funds** are available money in a bank account.

greet [V-T-U13] To **greet** a person is to welcome him or her.

handle [V-T-U15] To **handle** something is to work with it.

head teller [N-UNCOUNT-U13] A **head teller** supervises other tellers.

hundred [N-COUNT-U7] **Hundred** is combined with another number to abbreviate numbers in the thousands. For example, the number 2,300 could be stated twenty-three hundred.

ink [N-UNCOUNT-U2] **Ink** is a colored dye used in pens and for making fingerprints.

interest [N-COUNT-U8] **Interest** is a percentage given when money is loaned.

interest rate [N-COUNT-U8] The **interest rate** is the speed at which interest accumulates.

introductory rate [N-COUNT-U10] An **introductory** rate is a low interest rate that is only available for a short time after a credit card user begins service.

inventory [N-UNCOUNT-U2] **Inventory** is the total amount of supplies in an office or business.

is [V-T-U7] If the answer to a mathematical problem **is** a number, it equals that number.

issue [N-COUNT-U14] An **issue** is a complaint or problem.

issue [V-T-U15] To **issue** something is to give it out.

less [PREP-U7] **Less** is used when taking a number away from another.

limit [N-COUNT-U8] A **limit** is the maximum number of times something can happen.

liquid [ADJ-U9] If something is **liquid**, it is made up of money or can be converted easily into money.

lobby [N-COUNT-U6] A **lobby** is an area at the entrance of a building.

lock out [V-T-U12] To **lock out** is to prevent a user from accessing an account online after a certain number of incorrect log in attempts.

log in [V-I-U12] To **log in** is to enter a username and password on a website to gain access to an account.

long-term [ADJ-U8] If something is **long-term** it exists for a long period of time.

maintenance fee [N-COUNT-U9] A **maintenance fee** is a charge for keeping an account with a particular bank.

manager's office [N-COUNT-U6] A **manager's office** is a room where a supervisor does his or her work.

mat [N-COUNT-U3] A **mat** is a flat section of material on which people walk, stand, or wipe their feet.

minimum balance [N-COUNT-U8] A **minimum balance** is the smallest amount of money that must be in an account to open it or avoid paying extra fees.

minus [PREP-U7] **Minus** is used when taking away a number from another.

mobile banking [N-UNCOUNT-U11] **Mobile Banking** is the act of conducting bank business on a mobile phone or other portable device.

money order [N-COUNT-U15] A **money order** is a written request for a certain amount of money to be given.

monitor [N-COUNT-U5] A **monitor** is a screen on which information from an electronic device can be observed.

multiplied by [V-PHRASE-U7] If a number is **multiplied by** another, it is added onto itself that number of times.

Glossary

online banking [N-UNCOUNT-U11] **Online Banking** is the act of conducting bank business on a computer through a bank's website.

over [PREP-U7] **Over** is used when dividing a number by another.

overdraft [N-COUNT-U9] An **overdraft** is an amount of money deducted from a bank account that exceeds the amount of money available to spend.

oversee [V-T-U13] To **oversee** a business is to be in charge of its day-to-day operations.

paperless [ADJ-U12] If something is **paperless**, it does not involve paper.

password [N-COUNT-U12] A **password** is a security code that protects private information and provides access to an account.

payment [N-COUNT-U15] **Payment** is an amount of money given or received.

pen [N-COUNT-U2] A **pen** is a writing utensil that uses ink.

phishing [N-UNCOUNT-U12] **Phishing** is the act of extracting sensitive information using fraudulent emails.

phone banker [N-COUNT-U14] A **phone banker** is someone who works for a bank making transactions over the phone.

PIN [N-COUNT-U11] A **PIN**, or personal identification number, is a secret code that someone uses with a particular debit card to access a bank account.

plus [PREP] **Plus** is used when adding two or more numbers.

post [N-COUNT-U3] A **post** is an upright cylindrical pole on a stand.

printer [N-COUNT-U5] A **printer** is an electronic device that makes a paper copy of information stored on a computer.

receptionist [N-COUNT-U13] A **receptionist** is an employee who greets visitors and answers phone calls.

records [N-COUNT-U13] **Records** are documents of information and transactions.

register [N-COUNT-U4] A **register** is a document that shows all transactions made through a specific account.

resolve [V-I or T-U14] To **resolve** is to find the solution to a problem.

returned [ADJ-U9] If a check or payment is **returned**, it is not honored by the bank.

rope [N-COUNT-U3] A **rope** is a narrow length of material stretched between posts to guide lines of people as they wait.

safe deposit box [N-COUNT-U6] A **safe deposit box** is a metal container in which valuable items can be locked.

savings account [N-COUNT-U8] A **savings account** is an account where people put their money and gain interest.

secure [ADJ-U12] If a payment is **secure**, it is safe.

security camera [N-COUNT-U5] A **security camera** is a camera used to record the activity of people.

security measures [N-COUNT-U12] **Security measures** are actions or devices that prevent theft.

shredder [N-COUNT-U5] A **shredder** is an electronic device that cuts paper into thin strips.

SSL [N-UNCOUNT-U12] An **SSL** is an encryption protocol that allows transmission of private data over the Internet.

stamp [N-COUNT-U2] A **stamp** imprints a specific word, phrase or image onto paper.

subtract [V-T-U7] To **subtract** a number is to take it away from another number.

support [V-T-U13] To **support** is to assist with a task.

swipe card reader [N-COUNT-U5] A **swipe card reader** is a device that reads information from the magnetic strip of a credit or debit card.

telephone banking [N-COUNT-U14] **Telephone banking** is a system where bank transactions can be done over the phone.

teller pedestal [N-COUNT-U3] A **teller pedestal** is a heavy duty box with locking drawers for organizing the money a bank teller collects and distributes.

teller receipt [N-COUNT-U4] A **teller receipt** is a slip of paper imprinted with the details of a bank customer's transaction with a teller.

teller station [N-COUNT-U6] A **teller station** is the counter where bank tellers process transactions.

times [PREP-U7] **Times** is used when multiplying numbers.

transaction [N-COUNT-U14] A **transaction** is an exchange of money.

transfer [V-T-U12] To **transfer** money is to move funds from one account to another.

vault [N-COUNT-U6] A **vault** is a well-guarded space where valuables are kept.

verify [V-T-U15] To **verify** is to make sure that something is true.

waiting area [N-COUNT-U6] A **waiting area** is a space with seating where people wait to be helped.

withdraw [V-T-U11] To **withdraw** money is to remove it from a bank account.

withdrawal [N-COUNT-U8] A **withdrawal** is the act of taking money from a bank account.

withdrawal form [N-COUNT-U4] A **withdrawal form** is a small sheet of paper someone fills out when he or she removes money from a bank account.

Career Paths

Banking

Book 2

Virginia Evans
Ken Gilmore, MBA

Express Publishing

Scope and Sequence

Unit	Topic	Reading context	Vocabulary	Function
1	Transfers	Website	account, address, bank-to-bank, electronic funds transfer, irrevocable, payment, routing number, RTGS, settlement, transaction fee, wire transfer	Explaining timelines
2	Loans	Website	application fee, apply, auto loan, borrower, closing cost, early-payoff penalty, financing, lender, loan, personal loan, principal, term	Defining financial terms
3	Home loans	Magazine article	adjustable rate, amortize, down payment, fixed rate, foreclose, foreclosure, home loan, mortgage insurance, mortgage loan, points, refinance	Explaining pros and cons
4	Certificates of deposit	Email	early withdrawal, initial deposit, insured, ladder, mature, mitigate, rate of return, reinvest, renew, return, variable rate	Making recommend-ations
5	Mutual funds	Advice column	average annual return, brokerage, commission, diverse, diversify, equity fund, invest, investment, management fees, money market fund, mutual fund, securities	Explaining risk
6	Retail banking: Community banks	Website	accessible, assets, character, community, community affairs, community bank, credit score, family, farmers, locally, on-site, risk averse, small business	Greeting customers
7	Retail banking: Commercial banks	Advertisement	business loan, commercial bank, construction, contractor, development, for profit, letter of credit, merchant banking, performance bond, secured loan, time deposit, underwriting	Gathering information
8	Retail banking: Credit unions	Letter	account holder, board of directors, common bond, credit union, eligibility, member, not-for-profit, World Council of Credit Unions	Disagreeing with an opinion
9	Investment banking: Front Office	Letter	acquisition, bond, debt capital, equity capital, insure, IPO, launch, merger, pitch book, proprietary trading, raise	Describing an increase
10	Investment banking: Middle Office	Textbook	capital, compliance, corporate treasury, credit risk, financial control, limit, market risk, middle office, operational risk, risk management, trader	Describing responsibilities
11	Investment banking: Back Office	Meeting minutes	back office, data-checking, information technology, operations, settle, software, state-of-the-art, technical support, trade, trade confirmation, trading algorithm, update	Talking about costs
12	Loan officer	Job listing	analyze, assist, bachelor's degree, creditworthy, economics, finance, loan officer, loan process, obtain, potential client	Describing customers' needs
13	Credit analyst	Website	cash flow, credit analyst, creditworthiness, evaluate, financial history, financial statement, meet, obligation, project, repayment, review	Expressing doubt
14	Branch manager	Job listing	branch manager, goals, grasp, hands-on, motivate, organization, oversee, relationship, responsible, solve, supervise, work ethic	Describing experience
15	Trust officer	Website	beneficiary, corporate trust, estate planning, fiduciary, investment, manage, performance, personal trust, portfolio, trust account, trust officer, trustee	Reassuring customers

Table of Contents

1 Transfers

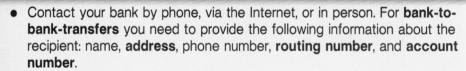

BANK SERVICES ▶ ELECTRONIC FUNDS TRANSFERS ▶ WIRE TRANSFERS

BANK OF THE NORTH

How do I complete a wire transfer?

- Contact your bank by phone, via the Internet, or in person. For **bank-to-bank-transfers** you need to provide the following information about the recipient: name, **address**, phone number, **routing number**, and **account number**.
- For transfers or **payments** to non-banking institutions or individuals, please speak with a representative in our member services department.

What does it cost?

- Standard wire transfer: $10 transaction fee
- **Real time gross settlement transfer** (RTGS): $25 **transaction fee**

How long does it take?

- Standard wire transfer: **settlement** within 2-3 business days
- RTGS: instantaneous

Can I stop a transfer?

- That depends on what type of transfer you used. Standard wire transfers can be halted prior to settlement. RTGS transfers cannot be stopped once initiated. All transfers are **irrevocable** after settlement.

Balance
7,708.78
7,765.42

bank-to-bank

Get ready!

1 Before you read the passage, talk about these questions.

1 What are the safest ways to send money overseas?
2 What are some differences between them?

Reading

2 Read the page from a bank's website. Then, mark the following statements as true (T) or false (F).

1 ___ Customers must contact member services for bank-to-bank transfers.
2 ___ A routing number is needed for all transfers.
3 ___ RTGS can be stopped within 2-3 business days.

Vocabulary

3 Match the words (1-6) with the definitions (A-F).

1 ___ irrevocable   4 ___ settlement
2 ___ account   5 ___ payment
3 ___ transaction fee   6 ___ wire transfer

A money sent electronically
B a place where money is stored
C money given for compensation
D money charged to transfer money
E the completion of a transfer
F unable to be stopped or changed

4 Fill in the blanks with the correct words and phrases from the word bank.

WORD BANK

electronic funds transfer   address
bank-to-bank   routing number
real time gross settlement

1 Provide your name, _____, and phone number.
2 There are different fees for each type of _____ .
3 Customers can only make _____ transfers.
4 Each bank's _____ consists of nine digits.
5 _____ guarantees an instantaneous transfer.

5 🎧 Listen and read the web page again. What is the quickest way to transfer funds between bank accounts?

Listening

6 🎧 Listen to a conversation between a customer and a teller. Check (✓) the events that are part of the wire transfer.

1 ☐ bank charges a fee from sender
2 ☐ recipient verifies account information
3 ☐ bank enters recipient's information
4 ☐ customer receives notification

7 🎧 Listen again and complete the conversation.

Customer: This is my first time doing this. So how does it work?
Teller: Well, first I'll need the recipient's name, contact information, and **1** _____ .
Customer: I have all of that information on a piece of paper.
2 _____ _____ _____ .
Teller: Thank you. **3** _____, I'll enter that into our system.
Customer: When will she **4** _____ the money?
Teller: After I submit the transaction, the funds should arrive
5 _____ _____ _____ .
Customer: Will I get a **6** _____ when the funds arrive?
Teller: Yes, once the funds arrive, you'll get an email notification.

Speaking

8 With a partner, act out the roles below based on Task 7. Then, switch roles.

USE LANGUAGE SUCH AS:

First, ...
After I ..., the funds ...
Once the funds ..., you'll ...

Student A: You are a bank customer who wants to do a wire transfer. Ask Student B about:
• information needed for a transfer
• costs of a transfer
• timeline of a transfer

Student B: You are a bank teller. Provide Student A with information about wire transfers.

Writing

9 Use the web page and the conversation from Task 8 to fill out the online form for a wire transfer.

BANK OF THE NORTH
Funds Transfer Instructions

Type of funds transfer: (Check one)
☐ **Between accounts**
☐ **Wire transfer**
☐ **Loan payment**

Transfer from: _____

Transfer to: _____

Provide additional information below:
_____
_____

2 Loans

Get ready!

1 Before you read the passage, talk about these questions.

1 What are some reasons people borrow money?

2 How do people borrow money in your country?

Reading

2 Read the page from a bank's website. Then, complete the table using information from the reading.

Loan Type	Restrictions on use	Term
Personal Loan		
Auto Loan		

Vocabulary

3 Write a word that is similar in meaning to the underlined part.

1 We can lend you an <u>amount of money</u> to purchase anything you want with just your signature. _ _ r _ _ _ _ l _ o _ _

2 Customers may <u>make a request</u> for a loan by contacting a member services officer. _ p _ _ y

3 The local bank offered him an <u>amount of money to borrow</u> at a very reasonable rate. _ _ a _

4 Jack paid a <u>fee for paying the remaining balance of his loan off before it was due</u>. _ _ _ _ y _ _ _ o _ _ _ _ _ _ l _ _

5 We will need to get an <u>amount of money to use toward the purchase of a new vehicle</u>. _ _ _ _ l _ _ _

6 The bank charged Wendy a <u>sum of money for requesting to borrow money from them</u>. _ _ _ _ _ _ a _ _ _ n _ e _

GREATER OAKTOWN BANK

Personal Loans

Individuals with good credit can obtain personal loans. All that is required is a signature. Borrow money for any purpose. Current **rates** are between 6.15% to 8.24%, depending on your credit score. Fixed 36 month **term**.

For more information visit one of our branch offices or call our customer help line at 1-800-555-4885.

Auto Loans

Do you need **financing** to purchase a new or used vehicle? We offer lower rates than many other **lenders**. **Terms** available up to 84 months. Qualified **borrowers** pay no **application fee**, **closing costs**, or down payment. Early payments may be applied directly to the **principal** of the loan with no **early payoff penalty**.

Call us at 1-800-555-4886 to find out about our current rates.

4 Read the sentence pair. Choose where the words best fit the blanks.

1 **lender / borrower**

A Send your payment to the _____ .

B A _____ can take out more than one loan.

2 **principal / closing cost**

A You pay a _____ when you sign a loan.

B Reduce the _____ by paying extra each month.

3 **term / financing**

A The loan has a _____ of 24 months.

B Many businesses need _____ to start up.

6

5 🎧 Listen and read the web page again. How many years does a borrower have to pay off a personal loan?

Listening

6 🎧 Listen to a conversation between a bank customer and a loan officer. Choose the correct answers.

1 What is the conversation mostly about?
   A inquiring about getting a loan
   B completing a loan application
   C understanding the details of a loan
   D negotiating the term of a loan

2 What will the customer most likely do next?
   A sign the loan
   B ask a question
   C make an early payment
   D complete an application

7 🎧 Listen again and complete the conversation.

Loan Officer:	Okay. 1 _____ _____ _____ the amount of the loan. In other words, it's how much you owe before interest.
Customer:	Oh, I see. So I have to pay that 2 _____ _____ .
Loan Officer:	Correct.
Customer:	Now, you said the loan has a term of 48 months. What's that exactly?
Loan Officer:	The term is 3 _____ _____ you must make payments on the loan. You'll pay a hundred and forty dollars a month for forty-eight months.
Customer:	Uh huh. Another thing I don't understand is this 4 _____ _____ _____ .
Loan Officer:	That is a fee we charge you if you 5 _____ _____ the balance of the loan before 48 months.
Customer:	Thanks for clearing that up. I'm ready to give it my 6 _____ now.

Speaking

8 With a partner, act out the roles below based on Task 7. Then, switch roles.

Student A: You are a customer approved for an auto loan. Ask Student B to clarify about:
● The term of the loan
● The monthly payments
● Any fees associated with the loan

Student B: You are a loan officer. Answer Student A's questions about the loan.

Writing

9 Use the web page and the conversation from Task 8 to fill out the loan offer. Make up some details.

GREATER OAKTOWN BANK

Loan Offer

Borrower: _____
Amount: _____
Type: (check one)
❏ personal ❏ auto ❏ other: _____
Term: _____
Fees: (explain in detail) _____
_____

Get ready!

1 Before you read the passage, talk about these questions.

1 How do people finance the purchase of a home in your country?

2 What are some costs associated with getting a home loan?

fixed rate

adjustable rate

Reading

2 Read the magazine article. Then, choose the correct answers.

1 What is the purpose of the article?
   A to suggest how to buy a foreclosure
   B to give advice to potential home-buyers
   C to advise buyers on avoiding paying points
   D to evaluate the risks and benefits of mortgages

2 Which is NOT a suggestion made in the article?
   A ask about early payoff fees
   B determine your budgetary needs
   C compare more than just interest rates
   D avoid buying bank-owned homes

3 What can you infer about fixed-rate loans?
   A They suit people who don't want to refinance.
   B They have fewer points attached to them.
   C They don't require mortgage insurance payments.
   D They are not suitable for buying foreclosures.

PERSONAL FINANCE - MARCH

How to Get the Mortage that's Right for You!

Considering a mortgage? Ask yourself these questions. How much can you afford for a **down payment**? How much can you pay each month? Answer honestly. Not doing so could mean having your home **foreclosed** upon in the future.

Next, determine if a **fixed rate** or **adjustable rate** mortgage is better for you. If you are willing to **refinance** down the road, an adjustable rate might be a good choice. Otherwise, consider a fixed rate.

When comparing home loans, don't just look at the rates. You also need to consider the costs of **mortgage insurance** and **points**. Talk with a loan officer if these are not clearly described. Ask if there is a penalty to **amortize** the loan early.

A note of caution: some lenders put restrictions on loans used to buy **foreclosures**. If this applies to you, talk with potential lenders before signing a loan.

Marvin Harrison

Vocabulary

3 Check (✓) the sentence that uses the underlined part correctly.

1 __ A We require <u>mortgage insurance</u> on all of our loans.
   __ B You can <u>amortize faster</u> by getting a higher rate.

2 __ A A <u>home loan</u> is needed for most housing purchases.
   __ B Apply at any location to <u>refinance</u> to buy your first home.

3 __ A Buyers are charged <u>points</u> when their payments are late.
   __ B The bank will <u>foreclose</u> after several missed payments.

4 Place the words and phrases from the word bank under the correct heading.

Word BANK

adjustable rate   refinance   points
down payment   fixed rate   amortize

Interest	Payment	Variation

5 🎧 Listen and read the article again. Why might somebody choose an adjustable rate mortage?

Listening

6 🎧 Listen to a conversation between a loan officer and a customer. Mark the following statements as true (T) or false (F).

1 ___ The buyer is not interested in adjustable rate loans.

2 ___ The buyer cannot make a 25% down payment.

3 ___ The buyer is unwilling to pay any points on the loan.

7 🎧 Listen again and complete the conversation.

Customer:	So what are my options for a 30-year **1** _____ - _____ mortgage loan?
Loan officer:	I have two for you. The **2** _____ _____ of the first is its low rate – 5.25%.
Customer:	Wow! **3** _____ _____ _____ .
Loan officer:	The rate is very low, but **4** _____ _____ _____ that it requires a 25% down payment.
Customer:	Ouch. That's **5** _____ _____ _____ . I don't' think I can afford that much.
Loan officer:	You can still get the loan, but we'll **6** _____ _____ _____ _____ .
Customer:	Hmmm. That's another **7** _____ _____ _____ . You said there was another option.

Speaking

8 With a partner, act out the roles below based on Task 7. Then, switch roles.

USE LANGUAGE SUCH AS:

The main advantage of ... is ...

The downside is ...

It requires a ...

Student A: You are a customer shopping for a mortgage. Ask Student B about:

● the interest rate

● points

● the down payment

Student B: You are a mortgage officer with two mortgage loan options. Talk to Student A about the pros and cons of each option.

Writing

9 Use the article and the conversation from Task 8 to fill out the customer interest form.

CUSTOMER INTEREST FORM

Mortgage Loan Division

What type of mortgage are you looking for? (Check one) ❏ fixed rate ❏ adjustable rate

What term? ❏ 30 year ❏ 15 year

How much do you have available for a down payment? _____

Are you willing to pay points? _____

What is more important to you: low points, low rate, low down payment? Explain. _____
_____
_____

|2011|2012|2013|2014|2015|2016|2017|2018|2019|2020|

variable rate

3 MONTHS

6 MONTHS

1 YEAR

2 YEARS

ladder

reinvest

1.25%

rate of return

To: Sales Staff
From: Charles Prine
Date: March 11
Subject: New CD products

Dear Staff:

Here are our newest **Certificate of Deposit (CD)** products. Please familiarize yourself with the following information and communicate the changes to customers.

Certificate of Deposits (fixed rate / FDIC **insured**)

Term	Rate of return
1 year	1.12%
2 years	1.95%
5 years	2.85%

Certificates of Deposits (**variable rate** / un-insured)

Term	Current rate of return
1 year	1.87%
2 years	2.65%
5 years	3.55%

Note: Minimum **initial deposit** for all CD products is $1000. Interest is paid monthly with the option to **reinvest** or receive payment.

Good communication with customers is essential to our continued business. Be sure customers understand the risk associated with our different products. All can be included in a **ladder** to **mitigate** risk. Clearly inform customers that when the CD **matures** they have the option to **roll over** or **renew**. Also, stress that if customers make an **early withdrawal**, they forfeit their **return** as a penalty.

Charles Prine, Manager, Hudson Bank

Get ready!

❶ Before you read the passage, talk about these questions.

1 How do people invest their savings in your country?
2 What are some investments that banks offer?

Reading

❷ Read the email from a bank manager to his sales staff. Then, mark the following statements as true (T) or false (F).

1 __ Customers can renew a mature CD.
2 __ Uninsured CDs cannot be put in a ladder.
3 __ Investors can receive monthly interest payments.

Vocabulary

❸ Match the words (1-6) with the definitions (A-F).

1 __ rate of return
2 __ mature
3 __ renew
4 __ reinvest
5 __ return
6 __ initial deposit

A the gain on a CD as a proportion
B the money paid on an investment
C to agree to buy a CD again
D the money spent to purchase an investment
E to put gains back into an investment
F to reach the end of a term

4 Fill in the blanks with the correct words and phrases from the word bank.

mitigate   insured   Certificate of Deposit
early withdrawal   ladder   variable rate

1   The return on a(n) _____ investment is uncertain.

2   Avoid _____ if you don't want to be penalized.

3   _____ CDs are a very safe investment.

4   With a(n) _____, the CDs mature at different times.

5   Conservative investors want to _____ risk.

6   You can purchase a(n) _____ that matures in 5 years.

5 🎧 Listen and read the email again. What is the smallest amount someone can invest in a CD?

Listening

6 🎧 Listen to a conversation between a customer and an advisor. Check (✓) the items the advisor recommends.

1 ❑ variable rate CD   3 ❑ a ladder
2 ❑ fixed rate CD   4 ❑ renewing the CD

7 🎧 Listen again and complete the conversation.

Customer:	So, I'd like to invest in a CD. And I don't want the **1** _____ to change.
Advisor:	I'd suggest a **2** _____ _____ CD then.
Customer:	Oh, and there is another thing.
Advisor:	Sure, what is it?
Customer:	I need some of my money available in **3** _____ _____ _____ _____ . The rest I won't need for some time.
Advisor:	In that case, **4** _____ _____ _____ _____ . I'd structure your CDs in a **5** _____ .
Customer:	What's that exactly?
Advisor:	Well, you invest some in a one year CD, some in a two year CD, some in a five or ten year CD. You **6** _____ _____ _____ .
Customer:	I see. What's the advantage of that?
Advisor:	CDs with longer terms pay a higher return. So you get a higher rate of return overall.

Speaking

8 With a partner, act out the roles below based on Task 7. Then, switch roles.

USE LANGUAGE SUCH AS:

I'd suggest …

Here's what I'd do …

I see …

Student A: You are interested in CDs. Talk to Student B about:
*   the type of rate you want
*   how long you want to invest
*   access to money

Student B: You are an advisor. Advise Student A on his or her investment options.

Writing

9 Use the email and the conversation from Task 8 to fill out the CD application form.

👥 **PEOPLES BANK**

Application for a Certificate of Deposit

Name: _____

Amount: _____

How many CDs do you wish to purchase? (Specify amounts, terms, and rates) _____
_____

Would you like any of your CDs to be automatically renewed when they mature? (If yes, specify which ones).
_____
_____

11

Get ready!

❶ Before you read the passage, talk about these questions.

1 How do people view the stock market in your country?

2 What are some ways people invest in the stock market?

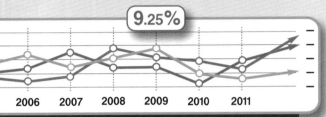

9.25%

2006   2007   2008   2009   2010   2011

average annual return

Money $ense

by Paul Horace

Everyday I get emails from people asking me where they should **invest** their money. Their situations are never quite the same, yet I almost always suggest mutual funds. Why? They are generally good **investments**. I like mutual funds because they allow you to **diversify** in different companies and even different types of **securities**. There is a **diverse** set of offerings: bond funds, **equity funds**, even **money market funds**. There is a fund for everyone.

Here are a couple of things to remember when shopping for mutual funds. First, decide how much risk you can handle. Money market funds are the least risky. Equity funds carry the most risk. Bond funds fall in between. Second, don't just compare **average annual returns**. A fund with a higher return might also have higher **management fees**. Third, choose funds from **brokerages** that don't charge high **commissions**. That can save you a bundle if you buy and sell frequently.

Reading

❷ Read the page from a financial advice column and the summary. Then, fill in the blanks with the correct words and phrases from the word bank.

wOrd BANK

costs   investment   commissions
investment types   risks

When people ask me, I often tell them a mutual fund is the best 1 _____ . They provide a wide array of 2 _____ . Some carry more 3 _____ than others. Don't just choose the fund that brings you the highest return. There are other 4 _____ to watch out for, such as management fees and 5 _____ .

Vocabulary

❸ Write a word that is similar in meaning to the underlined part.

1 Weigh your options carefully before you make a <u>choice to use money to earn profit</u>.   _ _ _ _ s _ _ _ _ t

2 The <u>knowledge of how much a fund earned over the past year</u> is important to investors.
   _ _ e _ _ _ _   _ _ _ _ _ l   _ _ _ _ r _

3 Stocks and bonds are two types of <u>financial products that can be used to make money</u>.   _ _ c _ r _ _ _ _ _

4 Many investors rely on the services of a <u>company that invests on the stock market</u>.   _ r _ _ _ _ _ g _

5 An easy way to increase savings is to put it in a <u>product that invests in many companies</u>.   _ _ t _ _ _   _ _ n _

6 People planning to retire should <u>use money to generate additional money</u> wisely.   _ n _ _ s _

❹ Read the sentence pair. Choose where the words best fit the blanks.

1 **diverse / diversify**
   A This broker offers a _____ portfolio of investments.
   B Mutual funds _____ your investments for you.

2 **equity fund / money market fund**
   A With a(n) _____, you can invest in stocks.
   B There is lower risk associated with a(n) _____ .

3 **commission / management fees**
   A Mutual funds typically charge _____ annually.
   B The broker earned a large _____ for the sale.

5 🎧 Listen and read the column again. Which is the riskiest type of mutual fund?

Listening

6 🎧 Listen to a conversation between a financial advisor and a customer. Choose the correct answers.

1 What is the purpose of the conversation?
  A to compare mutual funds
  B to promote a securities product
  C to give advice on buying a stock
  D to explain investment risks

2 What can you infer about the Vanadium Matrix Fund?
  A It is only sold on commission.
  B Its managers are inexperienced.
  C It hasn't lost money recently.
  D The advisor has invested in it.

7 🎧 Listen again and complete the conversation.

Customer:	I like the Vanadium Matrix Fund. Their average annual returns have been **1** _____ over the past ten years.
Advisor:	It's among the best funds. But remember, high returns are not guaranteed. Mutual funds, even the Matrix fund, can loose money if the **2** _____ _____ .
Customer:	Right, but don't past returns indicate **3** _____ _____?
Advisor:	In most cases, yes. But there's another thing to **4** _____ _____ _____ .
Customer:	What's that?
Advisor:	Some funds, like the Matrix Fund, charge high **5** _____ _____ .
Customer:	Oh. Does that **6** _____ _____ my return?
Advisor:	It sure does.

Speaking

8 With a partner, act out the roles below based on Task 7. Then, switch roles.

USE LANGUAGE SUCH AS:
But remember …
… don't past returns …?
… another thing to watch out for.

Student A: You are an investor shopping for mutual funds. Talk to Student B about:
● how much risk you prefer
● what kind of return you want
● how you feel about fees

Student B: You are a financial advisor. Help Student A understand the risks about buying mutual funds.

Writing

9 Use the column and the conversation from Task 8 to fill out the customer satisfaction form from a brokerage.

🐟 **Hamilton**

FISH FINANCIAL ADVISORS

Customer
Satisfaction Form

Customer's Name: _____

Financial Advisor: _____

What was the purpose of your visit? _____

What advice did you receive? _____

How would you rate the quality of the advice? Please explain why. _____
_____

●●● WINCHESTER
Community Bank

"Neighbors helping neighbors."

> About us

Since 1938, we have served the **community** of Winchester. We have proudly remained **locally** owned and operated. We serve families, **small businesses**, and farmers in the area. We offer loans, personal accounts, and business accounts.

We know that your **assets** are important to you. That is why we are a risk-averse institution. You can trust us with your savings. All of our accounts are insured up to $200,000.

We apply the same principals to our loans. We get to know our customer's needs and **characters**. We make decisions on more than just their **credit scores**. Loans are not one size fits all.

We aim to be **accessible** at all hours. That's why we offer ATMs, online banking, and phone services. You can also receive **on-site** service at any of our six branches.

From our early days, we have had an interest in **community affairs**. Our employees participate in local charities. Also check out our free financial education workshops.

farmers

small business

Get ready!

❶ **Before you read the passage, talk about these questions.**

1 Which types of bank are most popular in your country?

2 What are the advantages of smaller banks?

Reading

❷ **Read the page from a community bank's website. Then, choose the correct answers.**

1 What is the main idea of the reading?
- A to provide an overview of a bank
- B to explain different savings products
- C to discuss how a bank changed over time
- D to describe a bank's charitable activities

2 What can you infer about the bank's loans?
- A They are usually of a small amount.
- B They are insured against default.
- C They are personalized for the borrower.
- D They offer a reasonable interest rate.

3 What is true of accounts at the bank?
- A They have no fees.
- B They are high-risk investments.
- C They are insured to a certain limit.
- D They are only accessible at one branch.

Vocabulary

❸ **Match the words (1-6) with the definitions (A-F).**

1 __ locally   4 __ on-site

2 __ credit score   5 __ community affairs

3 __ community   6 __ assets

A a person's belongings

B in or at a location

C in the same general area

D a rating of one's ability to pay off loans

E a group of people with some connection

F events that involve or impact a group

4 Place the words and phrases from the word bank under the correct heading.

Word BANK

credit score   family   farmers   risk averse
small businesses   accessible   character

Bank Traits	Applicant Evaluation	Bank Customers
_____	_____	_____
_____	_____	_____
_____	_____	_____

5 🎧 Listen and read the web page again. What amount are the bank's accounts insured up to?

Listening

6 🎧 Listen to a conversation between a banker and a customer. Mark the following statements as true (T) or false (F).

1 __ The woman is applying for a loan.

2 __ The woman failed to pay back a previous loan.

3 __ The woman will open a checking account.

7 🎧 Listen again and complete the conversation.

Employee: Okay. Have you done business with us before?

Customer: Yes, I have. I took out an auto loan a few years ago.

Employee: Has it been 1 _____ _____?

Customer: Um, well, yes. But I had trouble 2 _____ _____ _____ last year. Is this going to count against me in any way?

Employee: It could 3 _____ _____ _____ . So let me see if I can find your account. What's your name?

Customer: Patricia Morrow.

Employee: Okay, Ms. Morrow, it says you were 4 _____ on three payments.

Customer: Was it that many?

Employee: That's what our records say. It'll hurt your 5 _____ _____ . But we can still offer you our 6 _____ _____ _____, just not any of our preferred products.

Speaking

8 With a partner, act out the roles below based on Task 7. Then, switch roles.

USE LANGUAGE SUCH AS:

Have you done business with us before?

Is that going to count against me?

We can offer you …

Student A: You are a customer. Talk to Student B about:
● opening a bank account
● your past business with the bank
● a loan you repaid late

Student B: You are a bank employee. Talk to Student A about what accounts he or she can get.

Writing

9 Use the web page and the conversation from Task 8 to fill out part of an account application.

Account Application

Name: _____

Account applying for: _____

Does applicant have current or former accounts? Y / N

If yes, describe account history: ____
_____

What accounts does applicant qualify for?
_____

Continental
COMMERCIAL BANK

A friend of Business

Frank is a **contractor**. Ten years ago he bid on a $5 million waterfront **development** project. It was a big move for Frank who, up to then, had worked mostly on small **construction** jobs. He needed to upgrade his equipment, so he came to us for a **business loan**. We gave Frank a **secured loan** to buy equipment. We also issued him a **performance bond**. He won the bid, and his business took off. Frank now hires contractors of his own. He turns to us for **letters of credit** and relies on our high-yield **time deposit** accounts to grow his savings.

Since 1904, we have helped thousands of businesses with their banking needs. We are a **for profit** institution with a wide array of experience ranging from loan **underwriting** to **merchant banking**.

VISIT OUR WEBSITE TO FIND OUT WHAT WE CAN DO FOR YOUR BUSINESS.
www.continentalbankingsolutions.com

construction

contractor

Get ready!

① Before you read the passage, talk about these questions.

1 What are some banking services businesses rely on?

2 How do banks guarantee business transactions in your country?

Reading

② Read the advertisement from a large commercial bank. Then, mark the following statements as true (T) or false (F).

1 __ The ad describes the bank's founder.

2 __ The bank offers loans for construction.

3 __ The bank does not make profit from its loans.

Vocabulary

❸ Check (✓) the sentence that uses the underlined part correctly.

1 __ A Construction is to take things apart.

__ B Development usually increases business activity.

2 __ A Business loans help companies grow.

__ B Underwriting helps a company repay a loan.

3 __ A Merchant banking serves the needs of families.

__ B A secured loan requires collateral from the borrower.

4 __ A A time deposit can only be purchased once a year.

__ B A commercial bank serves the needs of businesses.

5 __ A A for profit company wants to make money.

__ B A contractor loans money for building projects.

6 __ A Performance bonds are supplied by contractors.

__ B A letter of credit guarantees payment.

❹ Write a word that is similar in meaning to the underlined part.

1 Matrix Corporation relied on GMP Direct for all of its corporate financial services needs.
_ _ r _ _ a _ _   b _ _ _ _ _ _

2 Taking responsibility for repayment of the loans is offered by most major banks. _ _ d _ _ _ r _ _ i _ _

3 Traffic was very slow due to building projects.
_ o _ _ _ _ _ c _ _ _ _

4 Don't put money you need soon in a account that you can only access after a period of time account. _ _ m _   _ _ p _ _ i _

5 The plumber had a document that proved that he would complete the work he promised.
_ _ r _ _ _ m _ _ _ _   _ o _ _

6 They hired a person to oversee the process of building for the new construction project. _ o _ _ _ a _ _ _ r

16

5 🎧 Listen and read the advertisement again. How long has Continental Commercial Bank been in business for?

Listening

6 🎧 Listen to a conversation between a banker and a contractor. Choose the correct answers.

1 What is the purpose of the conversation?
   A to arrange repayment of a loan
   B to inquire about a potential contract
   C to arrange the details of a project
   D to apply for a financial product

2 What is the contractor concerned about?
   A experiencing construction delays
   B having difficulty obtaining a bond
   C spending more than he budgeted
   D providing additional information

7 🎧 Listen again and complete the conversation.

Contractor:	I'd like to apply for a performance bond for an upcoming construction job. We're putting up a small office building.
Banker:	Okay. What's the estimated budget for the project?
Contractor:	I've calculated $750,000.
Banker:	Is that the amount you want for the **1** _____?
Contractor:	Yes.
Banker:	And **2** _____ _____ is the project expected to last?
Contractor:	Our timeline is nine months. But I'm **3** _____ _____ _____, so I'd like the bond to cover that entire period plus three months.
Banker:	Okay. We can do that.
Contractor:	**4** _____ _____ will you be able to issue the bond?
Banker:	I'll need to send your information to **5** _____ . I usually hear back from them in five to seven days.
Contractor:	Great. Let's **6** _____ _____ what information you need.

Speaking

8 With a partner, act out the roles below based on Task 7. Then, switch roles.

USE LANGUAGE SUCH AS:

What's the estimated budget …?
Is that the amount you want?
How long is the … expected to last …?

Student A: You are a banker. Ask to Student B about:
● the project
● the budget
● the timeline

Student B: You are a contractor. Talk to Student A about a planned construction project.

Writing

9 Use the advertisement and the conversation from Task 8 to fill out the application form.

Continental COMMERCIAL BANK

Performance Bond Application

Name: _____

Company: _____

Amount of Bond: _____

Duration of Bond: _____

Describe the project: _____

board of directors

account holder

credit union

November 15

Dear Member,

December 18 is our next meeting of the **board of directors**. There are several items on the agenda. First, two seats are open for election. Members may vote at any branch location until December 10.

Second, the board will also be deciding on two important issues. We are considering **expanding** our **eligibility** for membership. When we opened, federal employees with a **common bond** came together and provided the **collateral** to establish the **credit union**. We have since grown considerably. The vote will be on whether to allow other state employees to become **account holders**. In addition, we are considering opening a new branch on the city's south side.

Members are invited to attend this important meeting.

Sincerely,
Tanya Bayard
President, UFCU

United Federal Credit Union

A **not-for-profit** institution established to serve the financial needs of federal employees

MEMBER OF THE WORLD COUNCIL OF CREDIT UNIONS

Get ready!

1 Before you read the passage, talk about these questions.

1 What types of banks are non-profit?
2 How can membership in a bank benefit customers?

Reading

2 Read the letter from a credit union. Then, complete the table using information from the reading.

Action	Who will do it
Vote for board members	1 _____
Decide on new branch	2 _____
Attempt to join the credit union	3 _____
Attend the meeting	4 _____

Vocabulary

3 Match the words (1-6) with the definitions (A-F).

1 __ member   4 __ WCCU
2 __ eligibility   5 __ collateral
3 __ common bond   6 __ expand

A a person that belongs to a group
B property to guarantee loan repayment
C being able to do or join something
D an international banking organization
E a connection between people
F to become larger

4 Fill in the blanks with the correct words and phrases from the word bank.

word BANK

account holder   board of directors
not-for profit   credit union

1 Hank keeps his money in a(n) _____ .

2 The _____ is elected by members.

3 Only a(n) _____ can make deposits.

4 Most charities are _____ organizations.

5 🎧 Listen and read the letter again. Who may join the credit union currently?

Listening

6 🎧 Listen to a conversation between two board members. Check (✓) the items they disagree on.

1 ❑ meeting with members
2 ❑ expanding their membership
3 ❑ expanding the credit union
4 ❑ how to finance expansion

7 🎧 Listen again and complete the conversation.

Board Member 1:	We have to decide on whether to 1 _____ _____ _____ .
Board Member 2:	I think it's 2 _____ _____ .
Board Member 1:	I have 3 _____ _____ .
Board Member 2:	Why? What do you think?
Board Member 1:	The founders of our credit union stated that its mission was to serve the needs of federal employees. So I think we should 4 _____ _____ _____ .
Board Member 2:	I think 5 _____ _____ _____ .
Board Member 1:	What are you suggesting we do then?
Board Member 2:	Well, we have an outstanding reputation, and not only among our members. Lots of people would love to join our credit union.

Speaking

8 With a partner, act out the roles below based on Task 7. Then, switch roles.

USE LANGUAGE SUCH AS:

We have to decide …
I have to …
I think that's a …

Student A: You are a board member of a credit union. Talk to Student B about:
● changing the mission
● expanding membership
● building a new branch

Student B: You are a board member of a credit union. Disagree with Student A.

Writing

9 Use the letter and the conversation from Task 8 to fill out the board member's notes.

Notes on Expanding Credit Union Membership

Why people want to join: _____
_____
_____

Reasons to expand: _____
_____
_____

Reasons not to expand: _____
_____
_____

United Federal Credit Union

A **not-for-profit** institution established to serve the financial needs of federal employees

MEMBER OF THE WORLD COUNCIL OF CREDIT UNIONS

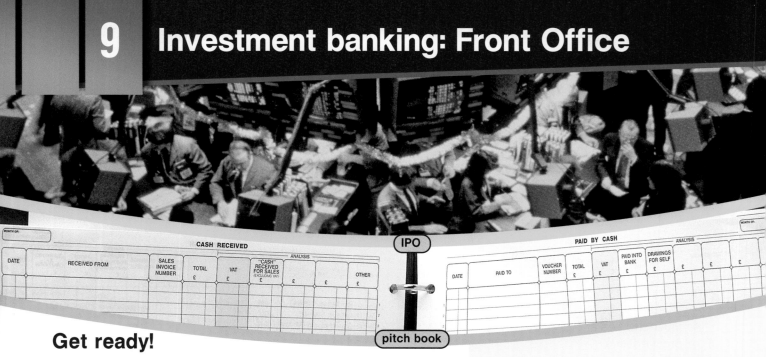

Get ready!

❶ Before you read the passage, talk about these questions.

1 How do companies increase their capital?

2 What are some types of work that investment banks undertake?

Reading

❷ Read the letter from an investment bank and read the summary. Then, fill in the blanks with the correct words from the word bank.

WORD BANK

expand obtaining **release** **profitable** working

Last year, the company assisted others in **1** _____ money from both equity and debt investment products. It also helped them **2** _____ new stock to the public. In-house traders had a very **3** _____ year. The company is **4** _____ with two companies that want to join together. It is also looking to purchase a financial services company and **5** _____ its services.

Vocabulary

❸ Check (✓) the sentence that uses the underlined part correctly.

1 __ **A** Public investors can do <u>proprietary trading</u>.

__ **B** <u>Raising</u> prices makes customers spend more.

2 __ **A** An <u>acquisition</u> allows investors to purchase stocks.

__ **B** The <u>pitch book</u> shows investment opportunities.

3 __ **A** The public can't trade company stock until the <u>IPO</u>.

__ **B** A <u>launch</u> is the purchase of another company.

4 __ **A** Many companies fail due to <u>debt capital</u>.

__ **B** <u>Insure</u> your investments to protect against losses.

5 __ **A** A <u>merger</u> combines two entities.

__ **B** Most companies purchase <u>equity capital</u>.

January 12

Dear Investor,

I'd like to take this opportunity to review last year's performance and our future plans.

We helped clients raise $15.2 billion in **equity capital** and $9.5 billion in **debt capital**. We successfully **launched** 96 **IPOs** for clients, 73% of which have grown more than 10%.

Our **proprietary trading** team earned excellent returns for the year. Our combined investment portfolio, including stocks, **bonds**, and private equity had a 13.7% return.

Looking at the year ahead, we are continuing to work with Franzita Corporation on their $6 billion **merger** with Ranger Enterprises. We are also working on an **acquisition** of Major Lux Financial Services. We are also planning to launch a new product which allows our clients to **insure** their investments.

There are many excellent opportunities ahead of us. We can prepare a customized **pitch book** to show you how to take advantage of them.

Happy new year!

Sincerely,
Garret Kemper, CEO, Golding Investment Bank

4 Read the sentence and choose the correct word.

1 We expanded our market share through the **acquisition / merger** of M3 Inc.

2 We made a profit on our **pitch book / proprietary trading** investments.

3 Jayson Inc. repaid its **bonds / equity capital** with a generous interest rate.

4 Rayburn Co. waited until January to **raise / launch** their new product.

5 KMP Inc. used $3.2 million in **debt capital / insure** to finance the project.

6 Stocks are one form of **equity capital / IPO** available on the market.

5 🎧 Listen and read the letter again. How much money did Golding Investment Bank raise for its clients in the previous year?

Listening

6 🎧 Listen to a conversation between a journalist and a banker. Choose the correct answers.

1 What is the purpose of the interview?
   A to explain the reason for a company merger
   B to inquire about a successful investment
   C to obtain investment advice on a company
   D to demonstrate how to increase stock value

2 Why did the banker invest in Kenyon Corp?
   A She knew the company president.
   B It had excellent stock returns.
   C She thought it would likely grow.
   D It was a popular investment.

7 🎧 Listen again and complete the conversation.

Journalist:	Could you give our readers **1** _____ _____?
Banker:	Sure. Last year, we found a **2** _____ _____ company, Kenyon Corp. It sells small batteries for electronics. **3** _____ was investing in them.
Journalist:	So **4** _____ _____ _____?
Banker:	We liked their product and saw they **5** _____ _____ _____ for huge growth. So we started with a $2.5 million investment in February. By May, it was worth $5.3 million.
Journalist:	And today?
Banker:	**6** _____ _____ _____ $10.2 million.

Speaking

8 With a partner, act out the roles below based on Task 7. Then, switch roles.

USE LANGUAGE SUCH AS:

We started with …

By …, it was worth …

It's now up to …

Student A: You are a journalist. Ask Student B about:
- an investment
- reasons for the investment
- profit on the investment

Student B: You are an investment banker. Tell Student A about a successful investment.

Writing

9 Use the letter and the conversation from Task 8 to fill out the journalist's interview notes.

URBANA FINANCIAL NEWS
Interview Notes

Interviewee: _____

Date: _____   Time: _____

Describe the investment: _____

How did they decide on that investment?

_____

How much did they make on the investment?

_____

risk management

credit risk

market risk

What is the Middle Office?

So far we have discussed the first of three logistical divisions in an investment bank, the Front Office. The second is the Middle Office. It concerns itself with three functions.

First, it is engaged in **risk management**. Employees calculate a variety of risk factors before allowing **traders** to finalize a trade. These include, but are not limited to, **market risk**, **credit risk**, and **operational risk**.

Second, it manages cash flows. In short, it is in charge of **financial control**. The **corporate treasury**, housed here, monitors all funds coming into and leaving the company. It also calculates profits and losses. In addition, employees ensure that the bank is in full **compliance** with government regulations and that its holdings exceed minimum **capital limits**.

The Middle Office usually also manages information technology resources. This involves ensuring the information infrastructure is up to date and working properly. In smaller firms, this function may be absorbed into the Back Office.

Chapter 9 ● page 144

Get ready!

❶ **Before you read the passage, talk about these questions.**

1 What are some risks investment banks face?
2 How can investment banks minimize those risks?

Reading

❷ **Read the page from a finance textbook. Then, complete the table using information from the reading.**

Middle Office Function	Example
1 _____ _____	Make sure computer systems are fully functional
2 _____ _____	Assess the potential for uncertainty caused by various factors
3 _____ _____	Watch over revenues and spending

Vocabulary

❸ **Read the sentence pair. Choose where the words best fit the blanks.**

1 **market risk / credit risk**
   A Falling stock prices are a _____.
   B A default on a loan is a _____.

2 **limits / capital**
   A Without _____, a company cannot spend money.
   B Governments set _____ on bank actions.

3 **compliance / financial control**
   A Banks must be in _____ with all laws.
   B Poor _____ can result in huge losses.

4 Read the sentence and choose the correct word.

1 The **corporate treasury / Middle Office** will update your software.

2 All orders to sell stock go through a **limit / trader**.

3 Errors caused by employees are a(n) **market risk / operational risk**.

4 The **corporate treasury / financial control** prepared a forecast.

5 Good **risk management / compliance** helps banks deal with uncertainty.

5 🎧 **Listen and read the page again. What Middle Office function is sometimes done elsewhere in smaller banks?**

Listening

6 🎧 **Listen to a conversation between a professor and a student. Mark the following statements as true (T) or false (F).**

1 __ The man misunderstands fiscal control.

2 __ Office technology is updated by the Middle Office.

3 __ The woman assigns the student more reading.

7 🎧 **Listen again and complete the conversation.**

Student:	Well, without a Middle Office, a bank couldn't **1** _____ _____ .
Professor:	Very good. That's **2** _____ _____ _____ _____ _____ . What are some others?
Student:	It's also **3** _____ _____ staying compliant with the laws, right?
Professor:	Yes. That's a very important function. But that's not **4** _____ _____ _____ _____ .
Student:	Um. I remember reading about **5** _____ _____ .
Professor:	Right. Did you understand what that meant?
Student:	Not exactly. I think it means that the Middle Office **6** _____ _____ _____ .
Professor:	Actually, that's incorrect. Fiscal control has to do with keeping track of the money coming into and leaving the bank.
Student:	Oh, yeah, I remember that.
Professor:	Good, good. Let's hear one last function.
Student:	The Middle Office is definitely in charge of managing IT resources. It makes sure technology is up to date.
Professor:	Excellent. You've obviously done your reading.

Speaking

8 **With a partner, act out the roles below based on Task 7. Then, switch roles.**

USE LANGUAGE SUCH AS:

Without a Middle Office …

It's also has the responsibility for …

Did you understand …?

Student A: You are a student. Talk to Student B about:
- risk management
- managing cash flows

Student B: You are a professor. Ask Student A about the responsibilities of the Middle Office.

Writing

9 **Use the page and the conversation from Task 8 to fill out the quiz.**

FINANCE 101
CHAPTER 9 - Quiz

1 What is one type of risk a Middle Office manages?

_____

_____

2 How does a Middle Office manage cash flows?

_____

_____

3 What is the third role of a Middle Office?

_____

_____

information technology

algorithm

software

Program v1.2
Program v1.3

WESTON Investment Bank

Back Office management
meeting minutes

Date: March 4

Attending: Theo Gray, Marylin Florida, Clive Harbin

Not attending: Yin Ping

Theo called the meeting to order at 9:01 am and handed out copies of the agenda.

Marylin **updated** the group on developments in the **information technology** division. Her team installed a new **software** program. It uses **state-of-the-art** trading **algorithms** and is projected to increase automated trading volume by 125%. This will free up traders to take on additional accounts. The program also automates 73% of the **data-checking** and **trade confirmation** functions of our office. We can now **settle** trades 25% faster. Some staff currently carrying out these functions will be transferred to other roles.

Clive reported that his team provided **technical support** to 136 clients over the past thirty days, an increase of 84.5% over last month. He requested permission to hire more staff.

Meeting adjourned at 9:58 am.

Get ready!

❶ Before you read the passage, talk about these questions.

1 What are some ways that investment banks rely on computers?

2 How have computers changed investing for the better? For the worse?

Reading

❷ Read the page from a bank's meeting minutes. Then, mark the following statements as true (T) or false (F).

1 __ The bank will reduce computerized trading.

2 __ Software will replace the functions of some back office staff.

3 __ Tech support would like to increase its personnel.

Vocabulary

❸ Match the words (1-6) with the definitions (A-F).

1 __ settle
2 __ update
3 __ trade

4 __ technical support
5 __ Back Office
6 __ state-of-the-art

A to get a more recent version

B the act of making an exchange

C assistance with technology

D being the most modern

E administrative section of bank

F to pay to complete a transaction

❹ Fill in the blanks with the correct words and phrases from the word bank.

WORD BANK

data-checking   trading algorithm   operations
information technology   trade confirmation   software

1 We need the _____ on the stock sale.
2 The _____ department maintains customer records.
3 The new _____ makes transactions automatically.
4 The program performs _____ for all records.
5 The _____ team updates our computers.
6 Install the _____ on all the computers.

❺ 🎧 Listen and read the page again. What will happen to those staff who are no longer needed to check data and confirm trades?

Listening

❻ 🎧 Listen to a conversation between two managers talking in a meeting. Check (✓) the items they mention.

1 ❑ Tech support has more work recently.
2 ❑ Tech support has become too expensive.
3 ❑ HR plans to hire a new employee.
4 ❑ Training costs less than hiring.

❼ 🎧 Listen again and complete the conversation.

Manager 1: We need at least one more employee.

Manager 2: How much would it cost to hire one?

Manager 1: I've estimated $65,000 per year including salary and benefits.

Manager 2: Have you talked 1 _____ _____ yet?

Manager 1: Not yet. I wanted to discuss this with you first.

Manager 2: Well, our budget is 2 _____ _____ _____ right now.

Manager 1: I understand, but we can't 3 _____ _____ _____ tech support.

Manager 2: I agree. So 4 _____ _____ _____ . Could we shift someone over from trade confirmation? The new software makes some of their functions redundant.

Manager 1: That could work. But we'll still have to pay for 5 _____ .

Manager 2: I'm sure that will 6 _____ _____ _____ than hiring an additional employee.

Speaking

❽ With a partner, act out the roles below based on Task 7. Then, switch roles.

USE LANGUAGE SUCH AS:

How much would it cost ...?

I've estimated ...

That would cost much less than ...

Student A: You are a tech support manager. Talk to Student B about:
- increases in your workload
- the need to for additional staff
- the costs of hiring and training

Student B: You are a back office manager. Talk to Student A about transferring an employee to save money.

Writing

❾ Use the page and the conversation from Task 8 to fill out the form to transfer an employee.

Weston Investment Bank - Back Office

Staff Transfer Form

Employee name: _____

Current team: _____

Team requested to transfer to: _____
_____

Reason for transfer: _____
_____
_____

Estimated cost: _____

loan officer

client

APPLY FOR LOANS HERE

10 Professionals Monthly - MARCH

LOAN OFFICER

Hiring company: Mason-Dixon Bank

Location: Cumberland, MD

Date of posting: March 6

Compensation: $35,000-$55,000 depending on experience - this is not a commission-based position

Job description: Meet **potential clients** and educate them on mortgage loan options available through Mason-Dixon Bank's mortgage loan division. **Assist** customers in all stages of the **loan process**: identifying appropriate loans, processing applications, **obtaining** loans, etc. **Analyze** loan applicant's financial profile in order to determine if an applicant is **creditworthy** or not. Direct existing customers seeking loan modification to appropriate professionals within Mason-Dixon Bank.

Candidate Qualifications: Must have a **bachelor's degree** in **economics** or **finance**. Minimum of three years experience in a mortgage origination office of a bank or other financial institution. Must have excellent oral and written communication skills. Working knowledge of financial software a plus; training provided otherwise.

Contact: Marshal Tucker, HR Manager, Mason-Dixon Bank, (310) 555-4000

Get ready!

1 **Before you read the passage, talk about these questions.**

1 What should someone do to obtain a loan?

2 What can prevent someone from qualifying for a loan?

Reading

BA in economics or finance

2 **Read the job posting. Then, choose the correct answers.**

1 What is the job posting mostly about?

A explaining the bank's mission

B outlining promotion opportunities

C describing the position's duties

D clarifying how to treat customers

2 What can you infer about the job?

A It is available to college students.

B It requires working with computers.

C It involves working at several branches.

D Good speaking skills are not necessary.

3 Which is NOT listed as a duty for this job?

A making modifications to a loan

B explaining different loan options

C helping customers decide on a loan product

D looking carefully at customers' finances

obtain

Vocabulary

3 **Check (✓) the sentence that uses the underlined part correctly.**

1 __ A Colleges award <u>bachelor's degrees</u>.

__ B <u>Potential clients</u> make up 90% of our accounts.

2 __ A If you are <u>creditworthy</u>, you will get the loan.

__ B To <u>analyze</u> loans is to collect payment.

3 __ A When you <u>obtain</u> a loan, you are done paying it.

__ B Applying is a step in the <u>loan process</u>.

4 Place the words and phrases from the word bank under the correct heading.

BANK

finance   analyze   loan officer   economics
obtain   potential client   assist

Individuals	Topics	Actions
_____	_____	_____
_____	_____	_____
		_____

5 🎧 Listen and read the job posting again. How much experience is required for the position?

Listening

6 🎧 Listen to a conversation between a job applicant and an interviewer. Mark the following statements as true (T) or false (F).

1 __ The woman used to work for Branson Bank.

2 __ The man feels that analyzing financial histories is the most important part of the job.

3 __ The man thinks that listening to customers lowers risk.

7 🎧 Listen again and complete the conversation.

Interviewer:	Well, your resume looks great. I see you worked with Branson Bank for five years?
Applicant:	I did. I started as a teller and ended as a loan officer.
Interviewer:	Okay. So, Mr. Hanks, tell me. In your experience, how important is **1** _____ _____ for a loan officer?
Applicant:	Oh, I'd say it's **2** _____ _____ _____ _____ of the job.
Interviewer:	Could you elaborate on that?
Applicant:	Well, if a loan officer **3** _____ _____ _____ a customer's needs, he could lead the customer into taking out the wrong loan. And that could be an **4** _____ _____ for the lender.
Interviewer:	Interesting. **5** _____ _____ .
Applicant:	A loan officer should be a **6** _____ _____ , otherwise he won't really understand the customer's needs.

Speaking

8 With a partner, act out the roles below based on Task 7. Then, switch roles.

USE LANGUAGE SUCH AS:

I see you worked …

In your experience …

Could you elaborate on that?

Student A: You are an interviewer. Talk to Student B about:

● job experience

● the role of customer service

● understanding customers' needs

Student B: You are a job applicant. Answer Student A's questions.

Writing

9 Use the job posting and the conversation from Task 8 to fill out the interviewers notes.

MASON-DIXON BANK
Employment Interview Notes

Date: _____

Position applied for: _____

Applicant's name: _____

How did applicant address the role of customer service? _____

How did the applicant describe customer needs? _____
_____

Other comments: _____
_____

Recommendation: _____
_____

Get ready!

1 Before you read the passage, talk about these questions.

1 What does a credit analyst do?
2 How do banks decide if they should lend money to an individual?

Careers in **Banking:**

credit analyst

Credit Analyst

review financial documentation

This is a job with a lot of responsibility. A credit analyst determines a potential borrower's **creditworthiness**. The borrower could be an individual or a company applying for a new loan or a line of credit.

Credit analysts must gather financial documentation about the applicant. This typically includes a **financial history** and, in the case of a company, the most recent **financial statements** and documented **cash flow**. The analyst then **reviews** the documents to formulate a clear picture of the applicant's income, assets, spending activity, payment history, and ability to **meet** additional debt **obligations**. The analyst does this in order to **project** the likelihood of **repayment**. Lastly, the analyst makes a recommendation to the loan or credit officer to either accept or reject the application.

Reading

2 Read this page from an employment website. Then, mark the following statements as true (T) or false (F).

1 __ The analyst prepares a financial history for the applicant.
2 __ A financial statement is used to determine creditworthiness.
3 __ The analyst makes the final decision on loan applications.

Vocabulary

3 Match the words (1-6) with the definitions (A-F).

1 __ cash flow   4 __ financial history
2 __ obligation   5 __ financial statement
3 __ repayment   6 __ evaluate

A to determine the value of something
B the spending and receiving of money
C paying back a loan
D something that must be done
E past behavior with money and expenses
F document of a company's financial activity

4 Fill in the blanks with the correct words and phrases from the word bank.

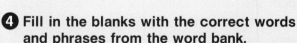

WORD BANK

creditworthiness   meet   project
review   credit analyst

1 The _____ recommended we give the loan.
2 Employees will _____ the application before making a decision.
3 The banks _____ greater earnings next quarter.
4 The Wilsons always _____ their debt requirements.
5 Because Joe lacked _____, he could not get a loan.

5 🎧 Listen and read the web page again. Whose ability to pay back loans does a credit analyst assess?

Listening

6 🎧 Listen to a conversation between a loan officer and a credit analyst. Check (✓) the items that describe the potential borrower.

1 ❑ sufficient capital reserves
2 ❑ strong cash flow
3 ❑ must pay higher interest rate
4 ❑ qualifies for smaller loan

7 🎧 Listen again and complete the conversation.

Loan Officer:	So, what is your assessment of their creditworthiness?
Credit Analyst:	Well, **1** _____ _____ _____ _____, they have adequate capital reserves.
Loan Officer:	Okay, that was my impression as well.
Credit Analyst:	However, I'm **2** _____ _____ _____ that it makes up for their insufficient cash flow.
Loan Officer:	Really?
Credit Analyst:	A company their size should be **3** _____ _____ at least 15% more revenue.
Loan Officer:	Okay, so **4** _____ _____ _____ rejecting their application?
Credit Analyst:	**5** _____ _____ _____ that's necessary. But I'd **6** _____ _____ .
Loan Officer:	Perhaps we can modify the loan. Maybe reduce the amount or raise the rate slightly.
Credit Analyst:	I'm not confident that a higher rate will make much difference in terms of risk.
Loan Officer:	I see.
Credit Analyst:	Your best bet is to discuss the possibility of a smaller loan, at least until they can increase their cash flows. If that happens, I can re-evaluate them.

Speaking

8 With a partner, act out the roles below based on Task 7. Then, switch roles.

USE LANGUAGE SUCH AS:

What is your assessment …?

Would you recommend …?

I'm not confident …

Student A: You are a credit analyst. Talk to Student B about:
● the applicant's cash flows
● the applicant's creditworthiness
● your recommendation

Student B: You are a loan officer. Ask Student A about the loan applicant.

Writing

9 Use the conversation from Task 8 to fill out the credit evaluation.

Credit Evaluation

Loan applicant: _____

Are the applicant's cash flows sufficient? Why? Why not?
_____
_____
_____

Is the applicant creditworthy? Why? Why not?
_____
_____
_____

Recommendation for applicant:
_____
_____
_____

29

14 Branch manager

Position: Branch manager

Date posted: May 3 **Company:** Golden State Bank

Duties:

- Responsible for **overseeing** day-to-day banking operations such as opening and closing customer accounts, performing wire and other electronic financial transactions, etc.
- Supervise and motivate tellers, loan officers, and other support staff
- Maintain accurate records and prepare weekly financial reports for the main office
- **Solve** customer, staff, and technical problems in a timely and **hands-on** manner with a minimal amount of disruption to banking operations
- Assist staff in setting performance-improvement goals and assess progress

Qualifications:

- Bachelor's degree in business related field
- Three or more years working as a branch manager or manager of a similar financial **organization**
- Working knowledge of word processing and spreadsheet software
- Firm grasp of electronic banking products and community banking principals
- Ability to maintain professional relationships with staff, clients, and customers
- A strong work ethic

Regional Manager

Branch Manager

Head Teller

Teller

staff

branch manager

Get ready!

❶ Before you read the passage, talk about these questions.

1 What are some of the things branch managers do?
2 How do branch managers interact with customers in your country?

Reading

❷ Read the online job posting. Then, complete the table using information from the reading.

Requirements	Duties
Education	1 _____
Work experience	2 _____
Professional knowledge	3 _____

Vocabulary

❸ Check (✓) the sentence that uses the underlined part correctly.

1 __ A <u>Branch managers</u> take instructions from tellers.
__ B Tom has a strong <u>work ethic</u> and works harder than everyone in the office.

2 __ A <u>Solve</u> the solution before you leave.
__ B His <u>goals</u> are to get a job and a house.

3 __ A Many business <u>relationships</u> are no longer face-to-face.
__ B <u>Hands-on</u> managers don't meet with clients.

4 __ A Managers <u>oversee</u> several employees.
__ B <u>Responsible</u> people often forget things.

5 __ A Commissions <u>motivate</u> salesmen.
__ B Managers must <u>solve</u> customers and employees.

6 __ A Clients often want to <u>supervise</u> managers.
__ B If you have a weak <u>grasp</u> of an idea, you don't understand it well.

4 Write a word that is similar in meaning to the underlined part.

1 Mr. Jenks must <u>watch over and check</u> the work of nineteen employees in his branch. _ _ _ _ r _ _ s _

2 Did you <u>fix</u> the computer problem? _ o _ _ _

3 Jack Tracy is <u>in charge of</u> for this office. _ _ s _ _ _ _ i _ _ _

4 Jon is an <u>actively involved</u> manager. _ _ n _ _ - _ _

5 <u>Successful groups of people working together</u> need good leadership. _ r _ _ _ i _ _ _ _ n _

6 Mrs. Keats was the <u>person responsible for a branch</u> for ten years. b _ _ _ _ _   _ a _ a _ _ _

5 🎧 Listen and read the job posting again. What must a branch manager do on a weekly basis?

Listening

6 🎧 Listen to a conversation between a job applicant and a interviewer. Choose the correct answers.

1 What is the conversation mainly about?

A inquiring about personality traits

B describing past work experience

C checking on educational requirements

D giving examples of solving problems

2 What is the applicant's current job?

A assistant manager   C bank teller

B operations manager   D branch manager

7 🎧 Listen again and complete the conversation.

Applicant:	I was a teller for two years before I was promoted to assistant manager.
Interviewer:	That's quite a quick promotion.
Applicant:	Well, the branch manager said she admired my work ethic.
Interviewer:	And what were you 1 _____ _____ in that position?
Applicant:	I performed many of the day-to-day operations 2 _____ _____ _____ _____ the branch manager. That lasted for about three years.
Interviewer:	Now your next position was as an 3 _____ _____ at headquarters?
Applicant:	That's correct. I held that position for a year, before I found an opening for a 4 _____ _____ position.
Interviewer:	Why did you 5 _____ _____ _____?
Applicant:	I like to have more hands-on interactions 6 _____ _____ .

Speaking

8 With a partner, act out the roles below based on Task 7. Then, switch roles.

USE LANGUAGE SUCH AS:

I was a …

Your next position …?

Why did you …?

Student A: You are an interviewer. Ask Student B about:

● previous jobs

● experiences in each job

● length of time at each job

Student B: You are a job applicant. Talk to Student A about your work experience.

Writing

9 Use the job posting and the conversation from Task 8 to fill out the job application form.

G Golden State Bank

JOB APPLICATION

Name: _____

Position applying for: _____

Experience: _____

_____

Qualifications: _____

_____

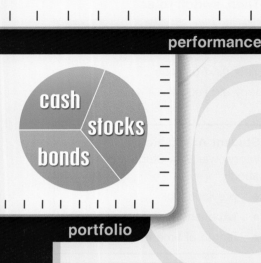

performance

cash
stocks
bonds

portfolio

© Greenfield Bank

Mark Pardo
Senior Trust Officer

Mark joined Greenfield Bank ten years ago as our senior trust officer. After obtaining degrees in law and accounting, he worked as an independent financial planner specializing in **estate planning** for fifteen years. He has extensive experience establishing **trust accounts**. Moreover, he has performed **fiduciary** responsibilities for thousands of individuals and companies. Mark and his team of junior trust officers are capable of setting up and **managing** both **personal trusts** and **corporate trusts**.

Mark's team can assist you in all of your estate planning needs:

- determining what assets to hold in your trust
- analyzing your **portfolio** to maximize the **performance** of your **investments**
- recommending tax-sheltered investments for your trust
- deciding on a **trustee**
- designating a **beneficiary** or beneficiaries
- acting as executor of an estate on a person's death

To set up an appointment, contact Mark Pardo at (505) 555-5005 or mpardo@greenfieldbank.com

Get ready!

❶ **Before you read the passage, talk about these questions.**

1   What happens to people's assets in your country when they die?

2   What tasks do trust officers undertake?

Reading

❷ **Read the page from a bank's website. Then, choose the correct answers.**

1   What is the purpose of the web page?
- A   to profile a recently retired trust officer
- B   to commend a bank employee
- C   to describe specific bank services
- D   to suggest products for a client

2   What can you infer about the trust officer's previous job?
- A   He managed a team of employees.
- B   He was involved in setting up trust accounts.
- C   He worked in another part of Greenfield Bank.
- D   He made investments on behalf of his employer.

3   Which of the following services is NOT mentioned?
- A   selecting who receives the trust assets
- B   purchasing investments for the client
- C   choosing a person to manage the trust
- D   determining how to make more money

Vocabulary

❸ **Read the sentence pair. Choose where the words best fit the blanks.**

1   **portfolio / investment**
- A   A CD is a very safe _____ .
- B   Mr. Kyle's _____ contains stocks and bonds.

2   **beneficiary / trustee**
- A   The _____ charges a one time fee for her services.
- B   Your _____ will receive the funds on your death.

3   **personal trust/ corporate trust**
- A   Mr. Parker created a _____ for his estate.
- B   The company established a large _____ .

4 Fill in the blanks with the correct words and phrases from the word bank.

estate planning	manage	performance
trust account	trust officer	fiduciary

1 The bank will _____ the account for me.
2 Our _____ can help you determine the beneficiaries.
3 Mr. Lee has _____ responsibilities for the account.
4 A _____ holds money for your children.
5 The _____ of stocks can be unpredictable.
6 _____ ensures your family gets your assets.

5 🎧 Listen and read the web page again. What types of trusts do Greenfield Bank manage?

Listening

6 🎧 Listen to a conversation between a trust officer and a client. Mark the following statements as true (T) or false (F).

1 __ The woman has no trust accounts set up.
2 __ The woman's children are her beneficiaries.
3 __ The woman will manage her own investments.

7 🎧 Listen again and complete the conversation.

Trust Officer:	We can do that. Okay, now what kinds of investments do you want to put in the trust?
Customer:	I'm not sure. I have some stock and bonds.
Trust Officer:	Both can be included.
Customer:	I want to make sure the portfolio grows. I'm worried there won't be enough money for each **1** _____ .
Trust Officer:	**2** _____ _____ _____ _____ . We can adjust your portfolio to meet your goals.
Customer:	Do you mean I need to **3** _____ some of my stock?
Trust Officer:	Not if you don't want to. But if you do we can handle the **4** _____ _____ _____ of any investments.
Customer:	**5** _____ _____ _____ . My husband left them to me. I'm not entirely comfortable managing them.
Trust Officer:	Don't worry. We'll **6** _____ _____ _____ you.

Speaking

8 With a partner, act out the roles below based on Task 7. Then, switch roles.

USE LANGUAGE SUCH AS:

What kinds of ...?

No need to worry.

We'll take care of you.

Student A: You are a customer. Talk to Student B about:
- your current investments
- your worries about your estate

Student B: You are a trust officer. Talk to Student A about how you can help him/her.

Writing

9 Use the web page and the conversation from Task 8 to fill out the trust account set up form.

◎ Greenfield Bank

Trust account holder: _____

Trustee: _____

Beneficiary(ies): _____

Current assets: _____

How would you like your assets divided?

_____

_____

How would you like your assets invested and/or managed?

_____

_____

Glossary

accessible [ADJ-U6] If a service is **accessible**, it is easy to reach or use.

account [N-COUNT-U1] An **account** is an agreement with a bank for it to hold your money.

account holder [N-COUNT-U8] An **account holder** is credit union member who has an savings or checking account with that institution.

acquisition [N-COUNT-U9] An **acquisition** is when one company buys another company.

address [N-COUNT-U1] An **address** is the location of a building including the street name, city, and other identifying information.

adjustable rate [ADJ-U3] If a loan is **adjustable rate**, the interest rate on the loan can change over the life of the loan.

amortize [V-T-U3] To **amortize** is to decrease the balance of a loan by making regular payments on it.

analyze [V-T-U12] To **analyze** is to study something in detail to understand it more clearly.

application fee [N-COUNT-U2] An **application fee** is money a potential borrower pays to apply for a loan.

apply [V-T-U2] To **apply** for a loan is to make a request for a loan.

assets [N-COUNT-U6] **Assets** are things that a person or company owns.

assist [V-T-U12] To **assist** is to help someone.

auto loan [N-COUNT-U2] An **auto loan** is a loan used to purchase a vehicle.

average annual return [N-COUNT-U5] The **average annual return** is a calculation that shows the percentage of profit or loss on an investment over one year.

bachelor's degree [N-COUNT-U12] A **bachelor's degree** is a level of education obtained from a college or university typically after four years of study.

Back Office [N-COUNT-U11] The **Back Office** is the part of an investment bank that is responsible for administrative support.

bank-to-bank [ADJ-U1] If a transfer is **bank-to-bank**, it goes from an account in one bank to an account in another bank.

beneficiary [N-COUNT-U15] A **beneficiary** is a person who receives money or property that has been entrusted to a trustee.

board of directors [N-COUNT-U8] A **board of directors** is a group of people that leads a corporation or other institution.

bond [N-COUNT-U9] A **bond** is an official document issued by an organization promising to pay back money it has borrowed from an investor plus interest.

borrower [N-COUNT-U2] The **borrower** is a person or business receiving a loan.

branch manager [N-COUNT-U14] A **branch manager** is the person responsible for managing a single bank location.

brokerage [N-COUNT-U5] A **brokerage** is a business where stock brokers work.

business loan [N-COUNT-U7] A **business loan** is money that is lent to a business.

capital [N-COUNT-U10] **Capital** is money or other assets used to start or fund a business.

cash flow [N-UNCOUNT-U13] **Cash flow** is the movement of money in and out of a bank or other business.

Certificate of Deposit [N-COUNT-U4] A **Certificate of Deposit** (CD) is a bank document promising its holder an interest payment on money invested after a specified period of time.

character [N-UNCOUNT-U6] **Character** is the combination of traits that makes up an individual's personality.

closing cost [N-COUNT-U2] A **closing cost** is money a borrower pays at the time a loan is given to them.

collateral [N-UNCOUNT-U8] **Collateral** is property that a borrower pledges to the lender as a guarantee in the event the loan cannot be repaid.

commercial bank [N-COUNT-U7] A **commercial bank** is a financial institution whose main function is to provide loans to businesses.

commission [N-COUNT-U5] A **commission** is money paid to a financial professional for selling a financial product.

common bond [N-COUNT-U8] A **common bond** is the set of social ties that connect the individuals in a group together.

community [N-COUNT-U6] A **community** is a group of people who live in the same area.

community affairs [N-UNCOUNT-U6] **Community affairs** are the issues and concerns of a specific group of people living in the same area.

community bank [N-COUNT-U6] A **community bank** is a bank that is locally owned and operated.

compliance [N-UNCOUNT-U10] **Compliance** is when someone obeys the rules.

construction [N-UNCOUNT-U7] **Construction** is the process of building houses, offices, bridges, and other structures.

contractor [N-COUNT-U7] A **contractor** is a person who organizes the building of a structure.

corporate treasury [N-COUNT-U10] **Corporate treasury** is a section of a company that manages its cash flows and forecasts future funding needs.

corporate trust [N-COUNT-U15] A **corporate trust** is a type of trust account created by a corporation.

credit analyst [N-COUNT-U13] A **credit analyst** is a professional who determines the likelihood of a borrower repaying a loan.

credit risk [N-UNCOUNT-U10] **Credit risk** is uncertainty caused by the potential for a borrower to not repay a debt.

credit score [N-COUNT-U6] A **credit score** is a number that measures a person's trustworthiness to pay their bills and debts.

credit union [N-COUNT-U8] A **credit union** is a cooperative financial institution that is owned by the people who use and operate it.

creditworthiness [N-UNCOUNT-U13] **Creditworthiness** is a characteristic concerning one's ability to repay a debt.

creditworthy [N-UNCOUNT-U12] If a person is **creditworthy**, a bank considers them a low-risk for receiving a loan.

data-checking [N-UNCOUNT-U11] **Data-checking** is the process of making sure information is valid and correct.

debt capital [N-UNCOUNT-U9] **Debt capital** is money obtained by a business through issuing bonds.

development [N-UNCOUNT-U7] **Development** is the process of causing business, commerce, and investment to grow.

diverse [ADJ-U5] If a mutual fund is **diverse**, it has many different types of investments.

diversify [V-Tor I-U5] To **diversify** is to invest your money in many different types of investment.

down payment [N-UNCOUNT-U3] A **down payment** is money that is paid toward the purchase of the home usually in order to qualify for a loan.

early withdrawal [N-COUNT-U4] An **early withdrawal** is the removal of money out of a CD before the CD matures.

early-payoff penalty [N-COUNT-U2] An **early-payoff penalty** is money a borrower pays if he or she pays off the loan before its term ends.

economics [N-UNCOUNT-U12] **Economics** is a field concerned with the production, distribution, and consumption of goods and services.

electronic funds transfer [N-COUNT-U1] An **electronic funds transfer** is a computer-based system used to perform bank transactions as distinct from transactions based on cash or checks.

eligibility [N-UNCOUNT-U8] **Eligibility** is the state of being qualified to receive something such as a loan.

equity capital [N-UNCOUNT-U9] **Equity capital** is the money invested into a business via stockholders.

Glossary

equity fund [N-COUNT-U5] An **equity fund** is a type of mutual fund that invests primarily in stocks.

estate planning [N-UNCOUNT-U15] **Estate planning** is the process of preparing for the disposal of a person's money and property when they die.

evaluate [V-T-U13] To **evaluate** is to make a judgment about something.

expand [V-T-U8] To **expand** something is to make it larger.

family [N-COUNT-U6] A **family** is a group of people who are related to each other through birth or marriage.

farmers [N-COUNT-U6] **Farmers** are agricultural workers who grow food.

fiduciary [ADJ-U15] If something is **fiduciary**, it relates to or involves the notion of trust typically in a professional capacity.

finance [N-UNCOUNT-U12] **Finance** is the field concerned with managing the flow of money.

financial control [N-UNCOUNT-U10] **Financial control** is the process by which an organization directs, measures, and monitors how its resources are used.

financial history [N-COUNT-U13] A **financial history** is the record of a potential borrower's income, investments, and debt.

financial statement [N-COUNT-U13] A **financial statement** is a document explaining an institution's financial transactions for a given period of time or the state of its finances at a particular point in time.

financing [N-UNCOUNT-U2] **Financing** is the act of providing funds to another person or institution for the purpose of their meeting a goal.

fixed rate [ADJ-U3] If a loan is **fixed-rate**, the interest rate on the loan does not change over the life of the loan.

for profit [ADJ-U7] If a bank is **for profit**, it aims to make money from its services and products.

foreclose [V-T-U3] To **foreclose** is when a lender takes possession of a home from a borrower due to nonpayment of the loan.

foreclosure [N-COUNT-U3] A **foreclosure** is a home that a lender foreclosed upon.

goals [N-COUNT-U14] **Goals** are things one plans to do or get in the future.

grasp [N-UNCOUNT-U14] **Grasp** is an understanding of something.

hands-on [ADJ-U14] If a person is **hands-on**, they get involved directly with fixing problems.

home loan [N-COUNT-U3] A **home loan** is a loan used to purchase a home (also known as a mortgage loan).

information technology [N-UNCOUNT-U11] **Information technology** is a field that deals with computers used for storing and retrieving information.

initial deposit [N-COUNT-U4] The **initial deposit** is the amount of money invested in a CD upon which interest is paid.

initial public offering (IPO) [N-COUNT-U9] An **initial public offering (IPO)** is when a corporation first offers the public a chance to buy its stock.

insure [V-T-U9] To **insure** is to contract with someone to give you money in the event that something bad happens to you or your investments.

insured [ADJ-U4] If a CD is **insured**, it has the backing of the government or other entity guaranteeing the holder against the loss of their investment.

invest [V-T-U5] To **invest** is to use your money to make more money by purchasing an investment such as a CD, mutual fund, stock, or a bond.

investment [N-COUNT-U5] An **investment** is something that you buy with the aim of increasing your money such as a CD, stock, or a bond.

investment [N-COUNT-U15] An **investment** is when money is used to gain more money.

irrevocable [ADJ-U1] If something is **irrevocable** it cannot be altered or stopped.

ladder [N-COUNT-U4] A **ladder** is a strategy for holding several CDs of different maturity dates.

launch [N-COUNT-U9] To **launch** is to make a product or service available that was previously unavailable.

lender [N-COUNT-U2] The **lender** is a person or business giving a loan.

letter of credit [N-COUNT-U7] A **letter of credit** is a document from a bank that guarantees a buyer will receive a seller's payment in the correct amount and on time.

limit [N-UNCOUNT-U10] A **limit** is a point that cannot be passed.

loan [N-COUNT-U2] A **loan** is money that one person borrows from another person or institution.

loan officer [N-COUNT-U12] A **loan officer** is a bank professional who helps customers find and obtain loans.

loan process [N-COUNT-U12] The **loan process** is the series of actions a person does to obtain a loan.

locally [ADJ-U6] If a bank is owned **locally**, it is owned by people who live in the same general area the bank serves.

manage [V-T-U15] To **manage** a trust is to have direct control over it.

management fees [N-COUNT-U5] **Management fees** are expenses mutual fund investors pay to financial professionals for managing a mutual fund.

market risk [N-UNCOUNT-U10] **Market risk** is uncertainty caused by day-to-day changes in prices of securities.

mature [V-I-U4] To **mature** is when a CD has reached the end of its investment period, meaning that its holder can cash it receiving the initial deposit plus interest.

meet [V-T-U3] To **meet** a financial obligation is to pay it back on time.

member [N-COUNT-U8] A **Member** is a person who owns a share of a credit union.

merchant banking [N-UNCOUNT-U7] **Merchant banking** is a type of banking directed at serving large corporations and very wealthy individuals.

merger [N-COUNT-U9] A **merger** is when two or more companies combine into one.

Middle Office [N-COUNT-U10] The **Middle Office** is the part of a financial company that manages risks and information technology resources.

mitigate [V-T-U4] To **mitigate** something is to lessen its negative effects or risks.

money market fund [N-COUNT-U5] A **money market fund** is a type of mutual fund that invests in short-term debt securities.

mortgage insurance [N-COUNT-U3] **Mortgage insurance** is money that a borrower pays to protect the lender in the event that the borrower fails to repay the loan.

mortgage loan [N-COUNT-U3] A **mortgage loan** is a loan used to purchase a home (also known as a home loan).

motivate [V-T-U14] To **motivate** someone is to encourage him or her to do something.

mutual fund [N-COUNT-U5] A **mutual fund** is a type of investment product that allows investors as a part of a group to buy stock or bonds from several different companies.

not-for-profit [ADJ-U8] If an organization is **not-for-profit**, it does not aim to make money from its services.

obligation [N-COUNT-U13] An **obligation** is a requirement.

obtain [V-T-U12] To **obtain** is to get something.

on-site [ADJ-U6] If a service is **on-site**, it is available at the location you are talking about.

operational risk [N-UNCOUNT-U10] **Operational risk** is uncertainty caused by the day-to-day operations of a company such as equipment breakdowns and personnel problems.

Glossary

operations [N-COUNT-U11] **Operations** are the financial transactions at an investment bank which include trades and customer records.

organization [N-COUNT-U14] An **organization** is a group of people working together, usually formally, for a shared purpose.

oversee [V-T-U14] To **oversee** employees is to supervise them.

payment [N-COUNT-U1] A **payment** is money that is given in exchange for a good or service.

performance [N-UNCOUNT-U15] **Performance** is the measure of profit or loss generated by an investment.

performance bond [N-COUNT-U7] A **performance bond** is a document protecting a buyer against loss if a project is not completed by a contractor.

personal loan [N-COUNT-U2] A **personal loan** is a loan used for small purchase such as a computer or vacation.

personal trust [N-COUNT-U15] A **personal trust** is a type of trust account that is created for a person or persons.

pitch book [N-COUNT-U9] A **pitch book** is an analysis of investment opportunities used by investment banks to market their services to potential clients.

points [N-COUNT-U3] **Points** are a fee paid at the time a loan is signed with each point equal to 1% of the value of the loan.

portfolio [N-COUNT-U15] A **portfolio** is a group of investments owned by a single person or entity.

potential client [N-COUNT-U12] A **potential client** is a person who may be interested in purchasing your services.

principal [N-UNCOUNT-U2] The **principal** of a loan is the amount that a borrower must payback separate from interest on that loan.

project [V-T-U13] To **project** is to calculate how something will be in the future.

proprietary trading [N-UNCOUNT-U9] **Proprietary trading** is trading done by an investment bank for its own profit rather than for its customers.

raise [V-T-U9] To **raise** is to increase the quantity of something such as money for an investment.

rate of return [N-UNCOUNT-U4] The **rate of return** is the amount gained or lost in an investment after a period of time expressed as a percentage.

real time gross settlement (RTGS) [N-COUNT-U1] A **real time gross settlement** is a type of electronic funds transfer that happens right away as a single complete transfer that is irrevocable.

refinance [V-T-U3] To **refinance** a loan is to replace it with a new loan that offers a better interest rate and/or terms.

reinvest [V-T-U4] To **reinvest** money is to take the gain from an investment and invest it back into that investment vehicle.

relationship [N-COUNT-U14] A **relationship** is the way in which a manager interacts with clients.

renew [V-T-U4] To **renew** is to purchase the same CD again after it reaches maturity date.

repayment [N-UNCOUNT-U13] **Repayment** is the act of paying back money that you borrowed.

responsible [ADJ-U14] If a person is **responsible** for something, they are in charge of that thing.

return [N-UNCOUNT-U4] The **return** is the amount gained or lost in an investment after a period of time.

review [V-T-U13] To **review** is to look over something carefully.

risk averse [ADJ-U6] If a bank is **risk averse**, it tries to avoid taking risks.

risk management [N-UNCOUNT-U10] **Risk management** is the process of analyzing and responding to uncertainty in an investment decision situation.

roll over [V-T-U4] To **roll over** a return is to invest that return in another account or product.

routing number [N-COUNT-U1] A **routing number** is a number that identifies a bank and is used when making payments or transfers.

secured loan [N-COUNT-U7] A **secured loan** is money that is lent on the condition that the borrower provides collateral.

securities [N-COUNT-U5] **Securities** are financial instruments such as stocks or bonds that can be traded on a market.

settle [V-T-U11] To **settle** is to pay money owed to another person or entity.

settlement [N-COUNT-U1] A **settlement** is when money being transferred is actually delivered.

small business [N-COUNT-U6] A **small business** is a type of business that is privately owned and operated and has few employees and assets.

software [N-UNCOUNT-U11] **Software** is a program that tells a computer what to do.

solve [V-T-U14] To **solve** a problem is to find a way to fix it.

state-of-the-art [ADJ-U11] If a machine is **state-of-the-art**, it uses the best and most recently developed technology.

supervise [V-T-U14] To **supervise** is to watch over employees and make sure they are doing their job correctly.

technical support [N-UNCOUNT-U11] **Technical support** is a service that provides assistance for using or solving problems with technology.

term [N-COUNT-U2] The **term** of a loan is the time in which the loan must be paid back.

time deposit [N-COUNT-U7] A **time deposit** is a CD or savings account that funds cannot be withdrawn from before a certain time.

trade [N-COUNT-U11] A **trade** is a financial transaction that involves selling and buying a security.

trade confirmation [N-UNCOUNT-U11] A **trade confirmation** is a statement verifying that a trade took place.

trader [N-COUNT-U10] A **trader** is a person who purchases and sells securities, typically over the short term.

trading algorithm [N-COUNT-U11] A **trading algorithm** is computer program that conducts trades automatically based on changes in timing, price, etc.

transaction fee [N-COUNT-U1] A **transaction** fee is money that a bank charges you when it completes a transaction on your behalf.

trust account [N-COUNT-U15] A **trust account** is a bank account in which the money is held to be given later to a beneficiary based on an event or date.

trust officer [N-COUNT-U15] A **trust officer** is a banking professional that manages the money and property people have placed in trusts with the bank.

trustee [N-COUNT-U15] A **trustee** is a person who holds money or property for the benefit of another.

underwriting [N-UNCOUNT-U7] **Underwriting** is the act of taking responsibility financially for an activity in the event that it fails.

update [V-T-U11] To **update** is to obtain the most recent information or version of technology.

variable rate [ADJ-U4] If a CD has a **variable rate**, its rate of return can change between the time of the initial investment and when interest is paid.

wire transfer [N-COUNT-U1] A **wire transfer** is a type of electronic funds transfer from one institution or person to another.

work ethic [N-UNCOUNT-U14] A **work ethic** is the moral value placed on working hard.

World Council of Credit Unions [N-COUNT-U8] The **World Council of Credit Unions** is a trade association that supports credit unions from around the world.

Career Paths

Banking

Book 3

Virginia Evans
Ken Gilmore, MBA

Express Publishing

Scope and Sequence

Unit	Topic	Reading context	Vocabulary	Function
1	Private banking	Website	alternative, flat-fee, hedge fund, high net worth, investable assets, minimum value, private banking, real estate, sizeable, tax planning, wealth management, yearly percentage	Explaining benefits
2	Savings and loans, thrifts and building societies	Newspaper article	building society, conservative, home financing institution, mortgage loan, mutual savings bank, mutually held, risky, savings and loans, security, thrift, voting rights	Drawing attention to ideas
3	Islamic banking	Business guide	acceptable, bear, collateral, cost plus, exclude, Islam, Islamic banking, joint venture, leasing, loss, profit sharing, prohibit, Shariah, usury	Making comparisons
4	Central banks	Newspaper article	central bank, contractionary, exchange rate, fiat money, inflation, interest rate, legal tender, monetary authority, money supply, monopoly, price stability, reserve bank	Agreeing and disagreeing with opinions
5	Fraud 1: Check fraud	Tellers' guide	alter, check fraud, check kiting, circular kiting, combat, counterfeit, float time, forge, forgery, fraud, manipulate, paper hanging	Reporting suspicious behavior
6	Fraud 2: Credit and debit card fraud	Magazine article	card security code, card-not-present transaction, copy, credit card fraud, debit card fraud, deposit envelope, duplication, identity theft, intentional, overdraft, skimming, stolen	Confirming a customer's identity
7	Fraud 3: Accounting fraud	Newspaper article	accounting fraud, arrest, books, cover up, demand draft, fraudulent, payable branch, ring, solicit, uninsured deposits	Describing a series of events
8	Fraud 4: Internet fraud	Website	antivirus software, bogus, hacker, Internet fraud, legitimate, link, pharming, phishing, redirect, scam, spyware, SSL connection, traffic	Delivering bad news
9	Robbery	Newspaper article	apprehend, armed, camera, comply, demand, dye pack, getaway car, note, report, robbery, security guard, silent alarm, steal, threaten, unarmed	Describing a person
10	Competition	Magazine article	club account, compete, competition, deposit account, IRA, loanable funds, money market account, notice account, NOW account, variety	Explaining options
11	Types of risk	Textbook	collection costs, credit risk, default, financial risk, liquidity risk, market, market risk, operational risk, portfolio, prevent, security, trade, value	Giving examples
12	Asset quality	Letter	asset quality, cash equivalents, government bond, hard assets, loan quality, non-performing loan, percentage, property and equipment assets, safe, shield, short term, tie up, treasury bill	Talking about risk
13	Crises and runs	Blog post	bank crisis, bankruptcy, demand deposit, deposit insurance, financial crisis, lender of last resort, panic, prevention, run, suspension of convertibility, systemic	Reassuring customers
14	Regulation principles	Website	bank license, breach, capital ratio, compliance, full reserve banking, market discipline, minimum requirement, principle, regulation, regulatory, revoke	Explaining reasons
15	Regulation requirements	Website	capital adequacy, capital requirement, corporate governance, credit rating requirement, disclosure, financial reporting, manage, minimum reserve ratio, regulate, reserve requirement	Talking about future events

Table of Contents

Pinnacle Bank
PRIVATE BANKING SERVICES

You've worked hard for your wealth. At Pinnacle Bank, your **sizeable** assets will work for you!

We offer the world's most powerful banking services to **high net worth** individuals. If your **investable assets** exceed a **minimum value** of $750 thousand, you qualify. See if our wealth management program works for you.

Wealth Management Services - Pinnacle private banking means personal attention from the most successful financial professionals in the industry.

Non-traditional investments - You will have access to a world of **alternative** investment strategies you never knew existed. Our **hedge funds** are the most effective investments on the market.

Real Estate - Every responsible financial plan includes real estate investments.

Our real estate market specialists will manage all your property accounts.

Tax planning - Tax efficiency is a crucial aspect of smart investing. Our tax lawyers and accountants will be key members of your wealth management team.

Inheritance planning - Our estate planners will see that your legacy is gracefully organized and distributed. Your family is our family at Pinnacle.

*Payment for our premier private banking services is a **flat-fee** rate, based on a **yearly-percentage** of total investments.

Pinnacle Bank
PRIVATE BANKING SERVICES
Your Best Choice!

private banking

real estate

$2,000,000+

high net worth

$$\frac{\text{Investment} \times 8\%}{1 \text{ year}}$$

yearly-percentage

Get ready!

1 **Before you read the passage, talk about these questions.**

1 How is private banking different from other accounts?
2 What are hedge funds?

Reading

2 **Read the website for private banking services. Then, mark the following statements as true (T) or false (F).**

1 __ Private banking is available for all Pinnacle Bank account holders.
2 __ Tax planning services are separate from wealth management services.
3 __ The flat-fee rate depends on performance of investments.

Vocabulary

3 **Match the words (1-6) with the definitions (A-F).**

1 __ private banking   4 __ investable asset
2 __ sizable   5 __ high net worth
3 __ tax planning   6 __ alternative

A larger than average
B possessing assets worth over $2 million
C non-traditional
D financial services for wealthy individuals
E financial services to minimize tax payments
F money that can be invested

4 Fill in the blanks with the correct words and phrases from the word bank.

wOrd BANK

flat-fee   yearly-percentage   real estate
wealth management   hedge fund

1   This _____ uses expert investing strategies.

2   Sam's _____ investments include several apartment buildings.

3   The fee is based on a(n) _____ of the total investment.

4   For large assets like yours, I recommend a(n) _____ program.

5   We only charge a(n) _____ rate.

5 🎧 Listen and read the website again. Which part of the bank deals with passing on wealth to investors' children?

Listening

6 🎧 Listen to a conversation between a banker and a potential client. Check (✓) the items that the program includes.

1   ☐ low returns   4   ☐ tax planning
2   ☐ hedge funds   5   ☐ inheritance planning
3   ☐ significant risk

7 🎧 Listen again and complete the conversation.

Banker: Well, you do have the investable assets we require for enrollment. Are you aware of our wealth management options?

Client: I read about them on your website. But what makes your hedge funds better than others?

Banker: 1 _____ are highly individualized approaches to investing. It's the adaptable strategies of our expert investors that 2 _____ _____.

Client: What kind of returns 3 _____ _____ _____?

Banker: That depends on a number of factors. But they will be significant and 4 _____ _____.

Client: What about 5 _____ _____?

Banker: Tax planning, inheritance planning, 6 _____ _____ of the wealth management program.

Client: It sounds appealing.

Banker: How do you feel about the 7 _____ - _____ payment?

Client: I think it's reasonable.

Speaking

8 With a partner, act out the roles below based on Task 7. Then, switch roles.

USE LANGUAGE SUCH AS:

Are you aware of ...?

What kind of returns ...?

How do you feel about .../

Student A: You are a banker. Talk to Student B about:
● wealth management
● flat-rate payment
● investable assets

Student B: You are a potential client. Talk to Student A about a private banking program.

Writing

9 Use the website and the conversation from Task 8 to write a letter of acceptance into a private banking program. Include the new client's qualifying assets, services offered, and fees.

Get ready!

❶ Before you read the passage, talk about these questions.

1 What are some alternatives to commercial banking?

2 How do most people purchase homes in your country?

mortage loan

savings

THE MONEY NEWS- JUNE

Study Reports Safe Alternatives to Banks and Risky Investments

Jihn Clause

Disheartened investors are looking for a safe, reliable place to put their money. According to a recent study by the Gordon School of Economics, that place is **savings and loan association.**

Most savings and loan associations, also known as **thrifts**, are **mutually held** institutions. This means borrowers and depositors have **voting rights** regarding the organization's corporate decisions. S&L members can influence everything from their institution's board members to its financial goals. The study states that such participation greatly increases satisfaction among depositors.

Other good investment choices include **building societies** and government-chartered S&Ls known as **mutual savings banks**. These **home financing institutions** are granted permission by the Federal Reserve to offer higher interest rates to depositors. This measure aims to increase the availability of **mortgage loans** to homebuyers. But it also gives mutual savings depositors an upper hand over those of commercial banks.

S&Ls also offer more security than other investments. Depositing money in an S&L is like making a long-term investment in your local mortgage market. For **conservative** investors, this is an appealing alternative to **risky** investments in the stock market.

Reading

❷ Read the newspaper article. Then, choose the correct answers.

1 What is the purpose of the article?
   A to describe alternative investing institutions
   B to explain mortgage loan availability
   C to compare building societies and thrifts
   D to give home financing advice

2 What is the NOT a characteristic of an S&L association.
   A makes mortgage loans
   B invests in the stock market
   C mutually held
   D offers security

3 According to the article, what do most members of S&Ls have?
   A thrift
   B voting rights
   C mortgage loans
   D building societies

Vocabulary

❸ Place the words and phrases from the word bank under the correct heading.

 **BANK**

savings and loan   risky
building society   mutual savings bank
conservative   thrifts

Home Financing Institutions	Investing styles
_____	_____
_____	_____
_____	

4 Read the sentence pair. Choose where the words best fit the blanks.

1 mortgage loan / security

　A We took out a _____ to buy our house.

　B John values _____ in his investments.

2 mutually held / home financing institution

　A This _____ gives seventy mortgage loans a year.

　B The S&L is _____ by its members.

5 🎧 Listen and read the article again. What is having a deposit in an S&L equivalent to?

Listening

6 🎧 Listen to a conversation between an S&L representative and a potential customer. Mark the following statements as true (T) or false (F).

1 __ The S&L's interest rates are lower than a bank's.

2 __ Over half of the S&Ls lending goes to mortgage loans.

3 __ The woman decides to apply for a loan.

7 🎧 Listen again and complete the conversation.

Customer:	Hi. What can you tell me about your deposit accounts?
Representative:	Well, our investment philosophy is based on the financial interests and security of our members.
Customer:	How do you determine your members' interests?
Representative:	Our members have **1** _____ _____ to address issues of the institution's financial policies.
Customer:	Interesting. I've heard **2** _____ _____ _____ interest rates than commercial banks.
Representative:	We do. To strengthen funds in the mortgage market the government allows us to offer slightly **3** _____ _____ to our depositors.
Customer:	So, you use the money of your depositors to make **4** _____ _____?
Representative:	Yes. Seventy percent of our **5** _____ is for mortgages on homes right here in Highwood.
Customer:	Wow. So the money I invest would help the community.
Representative:	Essentially yes. Your deposits would be like investments in the community.
Customer:	I see. Are the investments safe?
Representative:	**6** _____ _____ other types of investing ours is very secure.

Speaking

8 With a partner, act out the roles below based on Task 7. Then, switch roles.

USE LANGUAGE SUCH AS:

Our investment philosophy is ...

I've heard you offer ...

Are the investments ...?

Student A: You are an S&L Representative. Talk to Student B about:

● your voting rights

● interest rates

● security

Student B: You are a potential S&L account holder. Talk to Student A about a deposit account.

Writing

9 Use the article and the conversation from Task 8 to write a Savings and Loan mission statement. Include, voting rights, mortgage lending, and member security.

7

3 Islamic banking

Islamic Banking 101
For International Investors

McCleod's Guide to International Business — by Stanley Roberts

Many firms are looking to enter into the world of international investing. For these, the Middle East can be a lucrative market to tap into. To be successful, however, there are a number of things investors must understand about **Islamic banking** practices. Followers of **Islam** are bound by the strict rules of **Shariah**, or Islamic law. These rules touch upon all aspects of Islamic life, including business and banking.

The principles of Islamic banking emphasize the concept of **profit sharing**. Both investors and borrowers share the benefits reaped from invested assets. Both parties also agree to **bear** the risk of **loss**. Another important aspect of Islamic banking is that

Shariah **prohibits** the practice of **usury**. For that reason, **collateral** also plays an important role in Islamic loan agreements. Often, the lender owns the property outright until the loan has been paid in full.

Business relationships in Islamic countries often take the form of a **joint venture**. It is common for an Islamic company to temporarily join forces with a Western firm. The two parties share control over a specific endeavor and enjoy mutual returns. Other **acceptable** business arrangements in the Islamic world include **leasing**, and **cost plus** contracts. However, all arrangements **exclude** businesses that are considered in violation of Islamic values, such as the pork and alcohol industries.

Costs:	$ 1,200	loss
Investment:	$ 1,000	
Total:	− $ 200	

Get ready!

1 Before you read the passage, talk about these questions.

1 What are some characteristics of Islamic Banking?

2 Do you think that charging interest is unfair? Why or why not?

Reading

2 Read the page from an international business guide. Then, mark the following statements as true (T) or false (F).

1 __ Shariah does not allow for profit sharing.

2 __ Islamic banks share losses with investors.

3 __ Islamic companies may not work with Western firms.

Vocabulary

3 Match the words (1-6) with the definitions (A-F).

1 __ exclude   4 __ profit sharing

2 __ Islam   5 __ cost plus

3 __ leasing   6 __ Islamic banking

A the worship of Allah and his prophet Mohammed

B banking in accordance with Shariah

C to leave out

D an agreement to pay expenses and more

E paying for use of assets over a period of time

F practice of distributing gains to all members of an agreement

4 Write a word that is similar in meaning to the underlined part.

1 The company took a <u>negative profit</u> on the costly product.
_ o _ _

2 All members must <u>carry the weight of</u> the loss. _ _ a _

3 The two companies came together in a <u>temporary business effort</u>.
_ o _ _ t _ _ _ t _ _ _

4 <u>The charging of interest on loans</u> is forbidden in Islamic banking.
_ s _ r _

5 Shariah <u>forbids</u> this type of agreement. _ _ o _ _ b _ _ s

6 The house served as <u>security</u> on the loan. _ _ l l _ _ e _ _ _

5 🎧 Listen and read the guide again. What businesses may not invest in Islamic countries?

Listening

6 🎧 Listen to a conversation between two bankers discussing a trip to the Middle East. Choose the correct answers.

1 What is the discussion mostly about?
A a mortgage loan
B profit sharing rules
C a recent business trip
D Islamic banking practices

2 How do Islamic banks profit from home sales?
A by collecting fees from agents
B by charging interest from buyers
C by creating joint ventures with home owners
D by selling homes at higher prices than they were purchased

7 🎧 Listen again and complete the conversation.

Banker 1: Hi Frank. **1** _____ _____ _____ your Middle East trip?

Banker 2: Yeah. I've been reading up on Islamic banking. It's going to be **2** _____ _____ _____ _____ over there.

Banker 1: Sounds like it. **3** _____ _____ _____ _____ _____, but interest is forbidden, right?

Banker 2: Yeah. But you can still make a profit in banking.

Banker 1: **4** _____ _____?

Banker 2: Well. For one thing, they deal with mortgages **5** _____ _____ _____ _____ here.

Banker 1: Oh yeah? **6** _____ _____ _____?

Banker 2: **7** _____ _____ lending money for interest, a bank just buys the property. Then it sells it to the buyer for a higher price.

Banker 1: I see. I've also heard there's a lot of **8** _____ _____.

Banker 2: Yep. That's the typical arrangement, profit sharing, and loss sharing.

Speaking

8 With a partner, act out the roles below based on Task 7. Then, switch roles.

USE LANGUAGE SUCH AS:

Correct me if I'm wrong, but …

For one thing …

Instead of …

Student A: You are a banker preparing for a trip. Talk to Student B about Islamic banking and:
● usury
● profit sharing

Student B: You are a banker. Talk to Student A about Islamic banking practices.

Writing

9 Use the guide and the conversation from Task 8 to write a description of Islamic banking practices. Include prohibitions, focuses, and methods of doing business.

Get ready!

❶ Before you read the passage, talk about these questions.

1 What is the role of a central bank?
2 What institution creates the money in your country?

inflation

Clement Reserve Takes Contractionary Measures

The **central bank** of the United Republic of Clement took measures this week to slow its economy's rate of **inflation**. While the president of Clement insists the measures will be effective, some economists are doubtful.

The Clement National Reserve was established as the country's **monetary authority** in 1982. Since then the **reserve bank** has made significant additions to the nation's **money supply**. Between 1997 and 2007 the CNR introduced over four million dollars to the Clement economy. Surprisingly, prices remained stable, until this year. Since January, the rate of inflation in Clement has skyrocketed. Consequently, the value of the **legal tender** has fallen dramatically. **Exchange rates** for the currency have reached the unprecedented level of 79 Clement dollars to one Euro.

Like most modern currencies, Clement dollars are **fiat money**, not backed by precious metals. This fact, combined with the CNR's **monopoly** on creating the currency, has allowed for this week's **contractionary** measures. The CNR hopes to reduce the number of dollars in circulation through increased **bond** sales. According to officials, this should re-establish **price stability**.

Critics of the measures indict the CNR for being too drastic. They insist that standard adjustment of **interest rates** would more effectively solve the problem.

Reading

❷ Read the newspaper article and the summary. Then, fill in the blanks with the correct words and phrases from the word bank.

word BANK

extreme	removed	currency
taken	central bank	inflation

The central bank of the nation of Clement has **1** _____ measures to reduce **2** _____ . The problem is a result of the **3** _____ introducing too much **4** _____ to the money supply. To stop the inflation, the monetary authority has **5** _____ some of the currency from circulation. Critics of the plan say it is too **6** _____ .

Vocabulary

❸ Read the pair of sentences. Choose where the words best fit the blanks.

1 **money supply / central bank**
   A The _____ lowered interest rates today.
   B The _____ includes all available funds.

2 **contractionary / interest rate**
   A A(n) _____ policy will curb inflation.
   B A high _____ effects the mortgage market.

3 **legal tender / monetary authority**
   A This bill is _____ in the United States.
   B The _____ stopped printing $2 bills.

4 Fill in the blanks with the correct words and phrases from the word bank.

w **O** **r** **d** BANK

fiat money   monopoly
exchange rates
reserve bank   inflation
price stability   bond

1 _____ is not backed by gold.

2 The firm had a _____ on the industry.

3 The _____ prints new bills every year.

4 _____ have not improved since April.

5 Inflation slowed, and _____ was established.

6 High _____ rates hurt the dollar's value.

7 The government promises to pay a certain rate for each _____ .

5 🎧 Listen and read the article again. How can a central bank reduce the money supply?

Listening

6 🎧 Listen to a conversation between two bankers. Mark the following statements as true (T) or false (F).

1 __ The bankers disagree about the central bank's actions.

2 __ The central bank is changing the interest rate.

3 __ The man expects prices to stabilize in a few weeks.

7 🎧 Listen again and complete the conversation.

Banker 1:	Exactly. They're selling a lot of bonds. I think it's a terrible idea.
Banker 2:	Oh, really? I couldn't disagree with you more. I mean, this inflation is out of control. They have to do something.
Banker 1:	I just think there are better ways to slow inflation.
Banker 2:	Well, what would you suggest?
Banker 1:	For one, they could adjust **1** _____ _____ . That's what they've done in the past.
Banker 2:	Sure, changing interest rates has worked in the past. But inflation has never been this high before.
Banker 1:	**2** _____ _____ . It's the worst we've ever had.
Banker 2:	That's **3** _____ _____ _____ the bonds are a good idea. They'll reduce the amount of money out there.
Banker 1:	Well, **4** _____ _____ _____ _____ _____ . They need to lower inflation soon.
Banker 2:	That I can **5** _____ _____ . Hopefully they'll get it under control in a few weeks.
Banker 1:	A few weeks? **6** _____ _____ _____ . I think it will take at least a year.

Speaking

8 With a partner, act out the roles below based on Task 7. Then, switch roles.

USE LANGUAGE SUCH AS:

I think ...

What would you ...?

... has worked before, but ...

Student A: You are a banker. Talk to Student B about:
- inflation
- price stabilization
- interest rates and bonds

Student B: You are a banker. Talk to Student A about efforts to curb the inflation rate.

Writing

9 Use the article and the conversation from Task 8 to write a newspaper article about the results of a contractionary monetary policy. Include the reason for inflation, efforts to stop it, and likely results.

Recognizing and Avoiding Fraud

One of your duties as a teller is to be on the alert for people **manipulating** our system. Each teller should familiarize him/herself with the following list in order to help **combat** fraud.

1. Types of Check Fraud

Forgery includes creating fraudulent checks and imitating signatures on checks. **Counterfeit** checks are **forged** using either advanced printing or scanning techniques. **Altering** of checks also occurs. Chemicals can be used to erase information written on a check. Then, new information is added.

What to watch for: stains or discolorations, changes in the font or hand-writing, a missing address of the customer or bank, a missing signature, a missing or unchanging check number, low check numbers (which may indicate that the account is new).

Check kiting occurs when money is put into an account during the **float time** to conceal fraud. Sometimes **circular kiting** is used to transfer non-existent funds between banks. In the end, banks lose money when no effort is made to transfer real funds back into the account during the float time.

Detection: keep transaction records up to date, watch for large withdrawals of funds shortly after a deposit, watch for low average balances.

Get ready!

❶ Before you read the passage, talk about these questions.

1 What are some methods of check fraud?
2 How can check forgery be detected?

Reading

❷ Read the manual. Then, mark the following statements as true (T) or false (F).

1 __ The check number can indicate the age of an account.
2 __ Check kiting is used to hide fraudulent behavior.
3 __ Low average balances are warning signs of forgery.

Vocabulary

❸ Match the words (1-5) with the definitions (A-E).

1 __ fraud   3 __ manipulate   5 __ check kiting
2 __ counterfeit   4 __ check fraud

A an act of fraud where funds are put into an account before the float time ends
B a general term for using checks illegally to gain funds
C the use of deceit to gain money
D to change something for a particular purpose
E an imitation of currency

❹ Fill in the blanks with the correct words and phrases: *forged, forgery, float time, combat, alter, circular kiting.*

1 The man _____ the checks using a sophisticated printing process.
2 Not all check fraud involves transferring funds back into accounts during _____ .
3 The manual supplied detailed directions on how to _____ fraud.
4 The _____ of the checks failed because they were discolored.
5 The man used a technique called _____ to fraudulently acquire large sums.
6 He used chemicals to _____ the checks.

5 🎧 **Listen and read the manual again. What should bank staff do to help detect kiting.**

Listening

6 🎧 **Listen to a conversation between a teller and a branch manager. Choose the correct answers.**

1   Which of these does the teller believe the customer is committing?

   A circular kiting
   C counterfeiting
   B altering checks
   D check kiting

2   Which of the following warning signs is NOT attributed to the customer?

   A He has a low average balance.
   B His account is less than a year old.
   C His checks are sometimes discolored.
   D He is moving funds between multiple banks.

7 🎧 **Listen again and complete the conversation.**

Teller: Well, I've noticed some **1** _____ _____ going on with a customer's account. I thought I should tell you.

Manager: I see. So **2** _____ _____ _____?

Teller: The customer is **3** _____ _____ back and forth between our bank and a couple of others.

Manager: So, you think he might be **4** _____ _____?

Teller: Circular kiting is what I was thinking. He writes checks for more than he has in his account with us. Then **5** _____ _____ _____ _____ he makes a deposit from another bank.

Manager: I'm glad you **6** _____ _____ _____ _____. Do you know his average balance?

Teller: **7** _____ _____ _____ .

Manager: And do you know how long the man has **8** _____ _____ _____ with us?

Teller: Yeah, I reviewed his account history. His checking account has been open for about five months.

Speaking

8 **With a partner, act out the roles below based on Task 7. Then, switch roles.**

USE LANGUAGE SUCH AS:

I noticed some suspicious activity ...
The customer is moving funds ...
I've reviewed his account history ...

Student A: You are a teller. Talk to Student B about:

● a suspicious account
● the type of suspected fraud
● account details

Student B: You are a branch manager. Talk to Student A about the account and how to handle the suspected fraud.

Writing

9 **Use the manual and the conversation from Task 8 to write a memo on a possibly fraudulent check. Include: warning signs, account information, and what steps to take.**

memo

From: _____

To: _____

Date: _____

Subject: _____

_____
_____
_____
_____
_____
_____
_____

13

Get ready!

① Before you read the passage, talk about these questions.

1 How do criminals commit credit card fraud?
2 How can people avoid credit card fraud?

Reading

② Read the article. Then, choose the correct answers.

1 What is the main purpose of this article?
   A to discourage use of ATMs
   B to encourage people to pay with cash
   C to explain the difference between credit and debit fraud
   D to teach people about card fraud and how to avoid it

2 Which is NOT stated in the article?
   A Criminals do not need to possess a card to commit fraud.
   B Card information can be stolen from honest businesses.
   C Debit cards are more secure than credit cards.
   D Purchases from reputable stores are less likely to lead to fraud.

3 According to the article, how can deposit envelopes be used in fraud?
   A Criminals copy account information from them.
   B Criminals deposit them without any money inside.
   C Criminals remove new credit cards being delivered in them.
   D Criminals steal money being deposited in them.

Vocabulary

③ Match the words (1-6) with the definitions (A-F).

1 __ identity theft   4 __ card security code
2 __ skimming   5 __ credit card fraud
3 __ duplication   6 __ card-not-present transaction

A a transaction made on the phone or online
B stealing funds using a credit card
C taking information from a credit or debit card
D the stealing of someone's identity
E numbers on a credit card used for security purposes
F the act of making an exact copy

Protect your Plastic

Credit and **debit card fraud** affect thousands of people every year. Today, people are more reliant on plastic than cash or checks, and criminals take advantage of people's willingness to share their spending information.

How does it work? - Credit and debit cards don't need to be physically stolen for fraud to occur. A technique called **skimming** involves copying information from the magnetic strip of a credit or debit card. This often occurs when criminals adapt card readers at legitimate businesses to **copy** the card information. Then, the information is used for **duplication** of the credit or debit card.

Furthermore, consumers often forget that purchases made online and by phone are not necessarily secure. During **card-not-present transactions**, only the **card security code** is required. Purchases can be made by someone who has copied the card information.

How to protect yourself:

● Never leave documents with your account information lying around. Doing so increases your risk of **identity theft** and debit or **credit card fraud**.

● Only release account information online or by telephone when you're dealing with a well-known company.

● Keep track of your transactions. Criminals with your debit card and PIN can **intentionally** deposit an empty ATM **deposit envelope** and remove the deposit amount plus any other funds. But you'll be responsible for the **overdraft** fees. Notify your bank of any irregular activity.

skimming

duplication

card not present transaction

card security code

identity theft

deposit envelope

4 Fill in the blanks with the correct words and phrases from the word bank.

word BANK

copying   deposit envelope
intentional   stolen
debit card fraud   overdraft

1 Withdrawing more money than one has results in _____ charges.

2 Account information should never be written on a(n) _____ .

3 The criminal committed fraud by skimming and _____ credit cards.

4 _____ is becoming a wide-spread problem.

5 If an act is _____, it is performed with a certain purpose in mind.

6 The man took steps to keep his information from being _____ .

5 🎧 Listen and read the article again. Which companies is it OK to give your account information to over the phone?

Listening

6 🎧 Listen to a conversation between a bank representative and a customer. Mark the following statements as true (T) or false (F).

1 __ The man calls to report a stolen card.

2 __ The security question asks about the man's mother.

3 __ The representative will cancel the man's card.

7 🎧 Listen again and complete the conversation.

Customer:	Okay. **1** _____ _____ _____ cherrytomato746.
Representative:	That matches what we have here. And the security question asks for your **2** _____ _____ _____ .
Customer:	**3** _____ _____ _____ Linda Tierney.
Representative:	Thank you, Mr. Harris. Yes, I can see here that there is **4** _____ _____ _____ going on with your account.
Customer:	Yeah. I still have my **5** _____ _____ though. It's not like it was stolen. Still, someone is using it in another state.
Representative:	Well, **6** _____ _____ _____ some of the information on the card was **7** _____ _____ _____ from a card reader. So that information can be used from anywhere.
Customer:	What can I do?
Representative:	Well, we'll cancel the card immediately. Then I'll connect you to our fraud prevention division to talk about the charges.

Speaking

8 With a partner, act out the roles below based on Task 7. Then, switch roles.

USE LANGUAGE SUCH AS:

My password is …
I still have …

Student A: You are a victim of credit card fraud. Talk to Student B about:
- security questions
- the evidence of fraud

Student B: You are a bank representative. Ask Student A security questions and talk about credit card fraud.

Writing

9 Use the article and the conversation from Task 8 to write a report on a case of credit card fraud. Include how the victim noticed the fraud, how the information was taken, and how you addressed the problem.

Get ready!

❶ Before you read the passage, talk about these questions.

1 What are some reasons a bank would alter their records?

2 How is accounting fraud carried out in your country?

Reading

❷ Read the newspaper article. Then, mark the following statements as true (T) or false (F).

1 __ The article offers advice for victims of a bank scam.

2 __ Clarence Stokes was arrested for demand draft fraud.

3 __ Account holders at Johnson United didn't notice any fraudulent activity.

Vocabulary

❸ Match the words (1-5) with the definitions (A-E).

1 __ solicit   4 __ accounting fraud

2 __ demand draft   5 __ uninsured deposits

3 __ payable bank

A a bank that can cash a deposit

B funds deposited to an uninsured bank

C to request

D misrepresentation of funds

E a legal copy of a check

Marion Sentinel April 3

Banking Fraud Revealed

Last February, three managers from Johnson United Bank were **arrested** for their participation in a **fraudulent** banking scheme. There are several charges against the **ring**, including **demand draft** fraud, collecting **uninsured deposits**, and **accounting fraud**.

The trial last Thursday and Friday showed that Johnson United Bank was never insured. They **solicited** deposits from customers and altered paperwork from other area banks to collect deposits. The scam continued for around two years and went unnoticed by account holders. It wasn't until November that B & C Trust, a **payable bank**, noted unusual activity.

B & C Trust became suspicious of the large number of demand drafts they received which were issued by Johnson United Bank. Clarence Stokes, a branch manager at B & C Trust, alerted authorities of what he believed to be demand draft fraud.

In an apparent effort to **cover up** their fraudulent earnings, the trio is accused of **cooking the books** at Johnson United. The false loan paperwork, they believed, would account for their fraudulent gains. "I don't know how the victims will be reimbursed," Stokes said, "but I'm glad these guys ran out of luck."

arrest

---

❹ Fill in the blanks with the correct words and phrases from the word bank.

word BANK

cover up   ring   arrested
cooking the books   fraudulent

1 The criminals misrepresented company gains by _____ .

2 The man was _____ and taken to the police station.

3 The woman wasn't able to _____ her role in the crime.

4 The _____ was busted by a group of undercover agents.

5 The _____ demand drafts were cashed at a payable bank.

5 🎧 Listen and read the article again. What did the three managers use details of false loans for?

Listening

6 🎧 Listen to a conversation between an investigator and a victim of bank fraud. Choose the correct answers.

1 How is Mr. Paulson involved in this case?

   A He was a victim of demand draft fraud.

   B He solicited customers for the bank.

   C He had money in an account with the bank.

   D He received false accounting information.

2 What did Mr. Paulson find suspicious?

   A smeared printing

   B missing paperwork

   C odd teller requests

   D changing account numbers

7 🎧 Listen again and complete the conversation.

Investigator:	Do you mind if I ask you a few questions about your knowledge of the Walton Associated fraud?
Victim:	Of course not.
Investigator:	Thank you, sir. First, **1** _____ _____ _____ _____ _____ with Walton Associated Bank?
Victim:	Well, about a year ago I moved to Springfield. Walton Associated was **2** _____ _____ to open new accounts.
Investigator:	And you **3** _____ _____ _____ with them?
Victim:	That's right.
Investigator:	Now, when you opened the account, did you notice **4** _____ _____?
Victim:	Little things. But at the time it didn't **5** _____ _____ .
Investigator:	What did you notice?
Victim:	Well, **6** _____ _____ _____ _____ . Like the printing was smeared and numbers had been changed.
Investigator:	Well, Mr. Paulson, you couldn't have known it at the time. But this forged paperwork was used to set up uninsured accounts.

Speaking

8 With a partner, act out the roles below based on Task 7. Then, switch roles.

USE LANGUAGE SUCH AS:

Do you mind if ...?

Did you notice ...?

You couldn't have known ...

Student A: You are an investigator. Talk to Student B about:

● an account

● suspicions

Student B: You are a victim of fraud. Talk to Student A about your experience with the bank.

Writing

9 Use the article and the conversation from Task 8 to write a newspaper article about accounting fraud. Include the types of fraud, the criminals, and who was affected.

https://
SSL connection

more...
link

How to avoid Internet fraud

hacker

pharming

Get ready!

1 **Before you read the passage, talk about these questions.**

1 What are some ways that criminals deceive people online?

2 How can you ensure that a website is safe?

Internet users are vulnerable to various threats to their privacy. Users of online banking must be especially careful about guarding personal information. You can protect yourself by understanding and recognizing different types of Internet **scams**.

BE CAUTIOUS ABOUT PROVIDING PERSONAL AND FINANCIAL INFORMATION. Scammers use **phishing** to make you think you are giving your details to a **legitimate** bank website. Ensure the web address matches the name of the correct website, especially if you got there via a **link** from an email. Some scammers use **pharming** to **redirect** website **traffic** to other pages. These **bogus** pages can appear very similar to bank websites. You might think you are accessing your account, but you are really giving your password to a scammer.

Also, learn how to recognize whether a website has an

SSL connection before sending any personal data. This will prevent **hackers** from intercepting the information that is being transmitted.

PROTECT YOUR PERSONAL COMPUTER. Downloading software from unfamiliar websites is risky. Some programs promise legitimate services, but they might be loaded with **spyware**. These secret programs allow scammers to access everything you do on your computer. They can even make changes to your computer and Internet settings. You can get **antivirus software** to protect your computer against unauthorized software.

Reading

2 **Read the website. Then, choose the correct answers.**

1 What is the purpose of the website?

  A to prevent Internet fraud

  B to describe online safety measures

  C to warn customers of online scams

  D to offer protection services against Internet fraud

2 Which is NOT a recommendation made on the website?

  A Send personal data only via SSL connection.

  B Ensure the correct website appears in the web address.

  C Use antivirus software to protect against spyware.

  D Avoid downloading software from the Internet.

3 According to the passage, what is a benefit of antivirus software?

  A It establishes SSL connections.

  B It recognizes legitimate websites.

  C It keeps a computer safe from spyware.

  D It stops downloads from unknown websites.

ripts, such a...

Norton AntiVirus

Alert : Malicious script detected

...dows Script Host Shell Object

antivirus software

Vocabulary

3 **Match the words (1-7) with the definitions (A-G).**

1 __ scam   5 __ pharming

2 __ bogus   6 __ legitimate

3 __ traffic   7 __ antivirus software

4 __ redirect

A not real or valid

B the number of people visiting a website

C real or trustworthy

D deceiving someone to make money

E a program that protects a computer

F to change the path of something

G redirecting users to fake websites

4 Fill in the blanks with the correct words and phrases from the word bank.

Word BANK

Internet fraud   spyware
link   SSL connection
hacker   phishing

1   A scammer intercepted the data that was sent without a(n) _____ .

2   The _____ in the email directed customers to a bogus website.

3   Sheila was arrested for _____ after she stole financial information online.

4   Steven's antivirus software detected _____ on his computer.

5   Paula changed her bank password after a(n) _____ accessed her account.

6   The scammer used _____ to make the customer believe he was a bank employee.

5 🎧 Listen and read the website again. Where on the Internet do you need to be particularly careful to avoid fraud?

Listening

6 🎧 Listen to a conversation between a bank representative and a customer. Mark the following statements as true (T) or false (F).

1   ___ The woman is calling to confirm an email.

2   ___ The woman did not make an online purchase with an electronic check.

3   ___ The woman accidentally revealed account information online.

7 🎧 Listen again and complete the conversation.

Representative:	What **1** _____ for you, Ms. McDonald?
Customer:	There's a mistake on my **2** _____ . It says I made an electronic check purchase online on December 5th. I've never used an electronic check.
Representative:	Did you recently give out any **3** _____ over the Internet?
Customer:	I don't think so. Well, I did send some details to your bank, but **4** _____ .
Representative:	What kind of details?
Customer:	The bank sent me an email asking for my account number and **5** _____ . It said the information was necessary to keep my account open.
Representative:	Well, **6** _____ this, Ms. McDonald, but that wasn't really an email from our bank.
Customer:	I don't understand. Who sent it?
Representative:	It must have been a phishing scam to access your bank account. Once you sent them your account information, they were able to make that purchase.

Speaking

8 With a partner, act out the roles below based on Task 7. Then, switch roles.

USE LANGUAGE SUCH AS:

There is a mistake …

Did you give out any …?

I'm sorry …

Student A: You are a bank representative. Talk to Student B about:
• an online purchase   • an email   • Internet fraud

Student B: You are a bank customer. Talk to Student A about an online purchase.

Writing

9 Use the website and the conversation from Task 8 to complete the bank representative's fraud report. Include the type of fraud and the likely cause.

19

camera

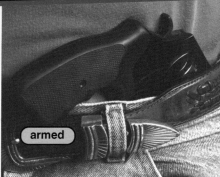

armed

Conklin Herald____A2

Police Catch Bank Robber

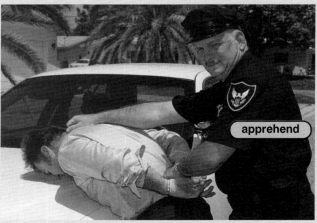

apprehend

Police were called to Conklin Bank on Thursday to address a **robbery** in progress. Police Chief Joe Ruskin said that robber attempted to **steal** hundreds of dollars in cash.

According to bank teller Monica Jameson, the robber entered the bank and handed her a **note** and a paper bag. The note ordered Jameson to fill the bag with money. It also stated the man was **armed** and prepared to shoot. He **threatened** to pull a gun from his jacket unless the teller **complied** with his **demands**.

Jameson secretly activated the bank's **silent alarm**, which notified the bank's **security guard** and local police of the situation. Jameson then filled the robber's bag with stacks of bills containing **dye packs**. Security cameras show that the robber then fled the bank in a **getaway car** driven by an accomplice.

Officers **apprehended** the robber trying to pass through a police roadblock. Upon searching the suspect, police discovered that he was actually **unarmed**.

Get ready!

❶ **Before you read the passage, talk about these questions.**

1 What are some ways people try to steal money from banks?

2 How do banks stop people from stealing money?

Reading

❷ **Read the newspaper article and the summary. Then, fill in the blanks with the correct words and phrases from the word bank.**

word BANK

security guard   paper bag   officers
bank teller   **gun   silent alarm**

The robber entered the bank and handed a note to the **1** _____ . It said he was carrying a(n) **2** _____ and ordered her to put the cash in a(n) **3** _____ . The bank teller triggered the bank's **4** _____, which notified the **5** _____ and police of a robbery in progress. The robber tried to escape in a getaway car, but police apprehended him. The **6** _____ discovered that he did not have a gun.

Vocabulary

❸ **Write a word that is similar in meaning to the underlined part.**

1 A witness <u>alerted the police</u> a robbery from her cell phone.
_ _ p _ _ _ e d

2 Albert went to jail for <u>the act of stealing something by threat of violence.</u>
_ _ b b _ _ _ _

3 Vern's police experience qualified him to work as a <u>person who protects a bank</u>.
s _ _ u _ _ _ y   _ u a _ _

4 The robber was <u>without a weapon</u>.
_ n _ _ m _ d

5 Tom was arrested for driving the <u>vehicle that the criminals used to escape</u>.
g _ _ _ w _ _   _ a _

6 The robber had a list of <u>orders</u>.
d _ _ a _ _ s

7 The officer was always <u>carrying a weapon</u>, even when he was off-duty.
_ r _ _ d

4 Read the sentence pair. Choose where the words best fit the blanks.

1 silent alarm / dye pack

  A The _____ ruined the stolen money.

  B The _____ alerted the guard that something was wrong.

2 threatened / stole

  A Henry _____ the man's wallet.

  B The officer _____ to shoot unless the robber dropped his weapon.

3 camera / note

  A Police used data from the security _____ to identify the criminal.

  B Julian did not want to threaten the teller aloud, so he wrote him a _____ .

4 apprehend / comply

  A The officer was disappointed that she failed to _____ the suspect.

  B Tellers should always _____ with robbers' demands.

5 🎧 Listen and read the article again. How did the police find out about the robbery?

Listening

6 🎧 Listen to a conversation between a police officer and a bank teller. Mark the following statements as true (T) or false (F).

1 __ The robber showed the teller a gun.

2 __ The teller was injured during the robbery.

3 __ The robber covered his face with a mask.

7 🎧 Listen again and complete the conversation.

Officer: Ms. Jameson, I'm sure you're upset. A robbery is a terrifying thing to go through. But do you think you could tell me what happened today?

Teller: Sure. A man came into the bank and gave me a note. It said he would shoot me if I didn't fill his bag with as much cash **1** _____ _____ .

Officer: Did you see the gun?

Teller: No. He had his hand in his **2** _____ _____ like there was a gun in there.

Officer: What **3** _____ _____ _____ then?

Teller: I started putting money in his bag, but I also pressed the button for the **4** _____ _____ with my foot.

Officer: Did he **5** _____ _____ in any way?

Teller: No, he **6** _____ _____ _____ . He just threatened me.

Officer: Can you describe him for me?

Teller: Sure. He had long, dark hair, brown eyes, and a mustache. He was wearing baggy jeans and a big jacket.

Speaking

8 With a partner, act out the roles below based on Task 7. Then, switch roles.

USE LANGUAGE SUCH AS:

... you could tell me ...

A man came into the bank and ...

Did he ...?

Student A: You are a police officer. Talk to Student B about:
- a robbery
- a suspect

Student B: You are a bank teller. Answer Student A's questions.

Writing

9 Use the article and the conversation from Task 8 to complete the police officer's incident report. Include a description of the robbery and the suspect's appearance.

loanable funds

Success in Banking

SAVINGS DEPOSIT

ACCOUNT NUMBER (10 DIGITS)
TELLER: PRINT TRANSACTION ON LINE 7

ID REQUIRED FOR CASH BACK
☐ PIN ☐ CC w/PIN ☐ DL OR

CUSTOMER SIGNATU

deposit account

5 | 1970 | 1975 | 1980 | 1985 | 1990 | 1995 | 2000 | 2005 | 2010

IRA

Although all banks store money, the **variety** of accounts and interest rates shows their diversity. Banks are like any other business. And like other businesses, banks must engage in **competition** to attract and retain customers.

In order to **compete**, banks have to provide incentives. They must have a good amount of **loanable funds** available to their customers and take some risks. For example, when the O & G Bank opened in March, they offered three standard accounts: **notice accounts**, **money market accounts**, and **IRA**s. Unfortunately, the bank closed only six months later. Simply offering services and products that customers can get at any bank isn't enough. It's important to stand out.

Had O & G Bank focused more energy on individualizing their services, their bank might have survived. Offering a variety of **deposit accounts** that suit customer needs improves customer satisfaction. **NOW accounts**, for example, are more flexible than many money market or notice accounts, and they earn interest.

Another aspect of personalizing services is increasing trust and intimacy between the bank and its customers. **Club accounts**, for example, are savings accounts geared toward a particular purpose. Helping customers plan for important events in their lives creates unity between the bank and client. And that connection can mean the difference between success and failure.

Get ready!

❶ Before you read the passage, talk about these questions.

1 What are some strategies banks use to attract customers?

2 How do different types of accounts address customer needs?

Reading

❷ Read the article. Then, mark the following statements as true (T) or false (F).

1 __ The author believes O & G failed due to the limited accounts it offered.

2 __ NOW accounts are deposit accounts that do not earn interest.

3 __ Club accounts save funds for specific uses.

Vocabulary

❸ Match the words (1-5) with the definitions (A-E).

1 __ competition   4 __ deposit account

2 __ NOW account   5 __ notice account

3 __ IRA account

A an account where notice has to be given prior to a withdrawal

B an account similar to a checking account that earns interest

C the process of attempting to succeed while others are making the same attempt

D an account where money can be deposited and withdrawn

E a retirement account where funds receive tax advantages

4 Fill in the blanks with the correct words and phrases from the word bank.

compete   loanable funds
variety   club account
money market accounts

1   The bank did not have many customers and could not _____ .

2   The woman decided to save for a vacation and opened a(n) _____ .

3   _____ is/are available for borrowing.

4   The business did well because it offered a _____ of services.

5   _____ pay different interest rates, depending on market conditions.

5 🎧 Listen and read the article again. What should O&G bank have done differently?

Listening

6 🎧 Listen to a conversation between a teller and a customer. Choose the correct answers.

1   What is the conversation mainly about?
   A account fees
   B interest rates
   C minimum balances
   D club account purchases

2   What kind of account will the customer likely open?
   A a club account
   B a NOW account
   C a deposit account
   D a money market account

7 🎧 Listen again and complete the conversation.

Customer: Well, I'm considering opening another bank account. I'm looking for something with a good interest rate.

Teller: All right. Well, 1 _____ _____ _____ _____ _____ _____ today, you'll receive point five percent yearly interest.

Customer: I see. The 2 _____ _____ _____ _____ offered a much better rate.

Teller: Okay. Well, 3 _____ _____ _____ _____ _____ would be better for you? Or a club account?

Customer: Which would you suggest?

Teller: If you're saving for 4 _____ _____ _____ the club accounts are a good option.

Customer: No. I don't have 5 _____ _____ _____ that I'm saving for besides retirement.

Teller: Okay. Well, our money market accounts typically offer good rates. 6 _____ _____ _____ though.

Customer: 7 _____ _____ _____ _____ around $16,000.

Teller: Oh, that more than meets the minimum.

Speaking

8 With a partner, act out the roles below based on Task 7. Then, switch roles.

USE LANGUAGE SUCH AS:

I'm considering …

Which would you …?

I'm hoping to deposit …

Student A: You are a bank teller. Talk to Student B about:
● opening an account
● interest rates
● a minimum starting balance

Student B: You are a customer. Talk to Student A about opening an account.

Writing

9 Use the article and the conversation from Task 8 to write an advertisement for a bank. Include the accounts offered, interest rates, and why customers should join the bank.

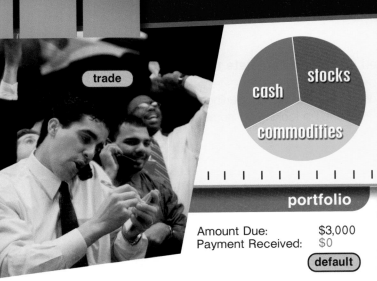

trade

portfolio

Amount Due: $3,000
Payment Received: $0

default

Get ready!

❶ Before you read the passage, talk about these questions.

1 What are some ways investors make money in your country?

2 What are some risks associated with investments?

Reading

❷ Read the book extract. Then, mark the following statements as true (T) or false (F).

1 __ All types of risk can result in profit or loss.

2 __ Collection costs prevent a security from losing value.

3 __ Liquidity risk includes situations where the market has no interest in a given security.

Vocabulary

❸ Match the words (1-7) with the definitions (A-G).

1 __ value
2 __ market
3 __ market risk
4 __ liquidity risk
5 __ financial risk
6 __ credit risk
7 __ collection costs

A any risk taken with financing

B a place where goods are exchanged

C the stated worth of something

D a risk that a portfolio will decrease in value

E a risk that an investor will lose money if the borrower doesn't make promised payments

F payments which allow for debt to be collected

G a risk that a security can't be traded quickly enough to prevent losses

Risks in Banking

Financial risks can greatly increase an individual's or company's wealth, or they can mean the loss of everything. The exception is operational risk, which does not involve gaining profit. **Operational risk** is a broad term that includes not only the banking world, but also any risk stemming from business functions. The following chapter details financial risks and the role they play in banking.

Overview:

Credit Risk is a risk taken by an investor. A **default** occurs when a borrower does not make promised payments. In this case, collection costs determined in a contract may come into play. **Collection costs** are a necessary aspect of financial risk because they **prevent** borrowers or debtors from taking advantage of an agreement.

Liquidity Risk is the risk that a **security** can't be **traded** quickly enough to make a substantial gain or prevent loss. This happens when nobody in the **market** has use for the security.

Market Risk is the risk that a **portfolio** will decrease in **value** because of the conditions of a market. There are four primary risk factors that affect the conditions of a given market: stock prices, commodity prices, interest rates, and foreign exchange rates.

❹ Fill in the blanks with the correct words and phrases from the word bank.

word BANK

traded   default   portfolio   prevent
security   operational risks

1 The _____ had low demand and value.

2 Mary couldn't make her payments, which caused her to _____ .

3 The conditions of the market affected the value of the company's _____ .

4 Collection costs _____ debtors from taking advantage of agreements.

5 Every business must address _____ .

6 Thousands of stocks are _____ daily.

5 🎧 **Listen and read the book extract again. How many types of financial risk does it discuss?**

Listening

6 🎧 **Listen to a conversation between a professor and a student. Choose the correct answers.**

1 What is this conversation mostly about?

   A how portfolios are affected by the market

   B how market risk and liquidity risk differ

   C how operational risks are beneficial

   D how profit is gained from securities

2 According to the professor, which of the following is true?

   A Liquidity relates to an entire portfolio.

   B Credit risk is similar to liquidity risk.

   C Operational risk is not a financial risk.

   D Market and liquidity risks are related.

7 🎧 **Listen again and complete the conversation.**

Professor:	Okay. 1 _____ _____ _____ _____ that you're having trouble with?
Student:	The different types of risks. Like 2 _____ _____ _____ _____ _____ .
Professor:	They have things in common. Maybe that's why you're confused.
Student:	Both mean that 3 _____ _____ _____ in value, right?
Professor:	Yes. The main thing to remember is that 4 _____ _____ _____ _____ _____ a portfolio.
Student:	Okay. So that's saying a group of investments will 5 _____ _____ _____?
Professor:	Yes. And a liquidity risk refers to the risk taken with 6 _____ _____ _____ .
Student:	So, that would be the risk that a 7 _____ _____ _____ _____ in value?
Professor:	That's one example. It's saying that any individual security might not get 8 _____ _____ _____ to prevent loss or to gain profit.
Student:	I see. So they're just two different types of financial risk?
Professor:	Right. The term financial risk includes operational, market, liquidity, and credit risks.

Speaking

8 **With a partner, act out the roles below based on Task 7. Then, switch roles.**

USE LANGUAGE SUCH AS:

What are the concepts …?

The main thing to remember …

The term … includes …

Student A: You are a professor. Talk to Student B about:

• types of risk

• risk similarities

• risk differences

Student B: You are student. Talk to Student A about questions you have regarding financial risks.

Writing

9 **Use the book extract and the conversation from Task 8 to write a summary of financial risks. Include types of risk, what they concern, and who they affect.**

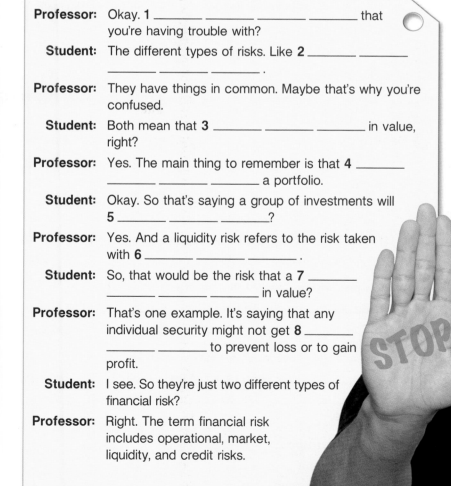

12 Asset quality

1/100 = 1%

CPA

hard asset

Cash	1%
Securities	12%
Loans	65%
Hard assets / P&E	22%

Carol Watson
CFO, Branson Bank

Mrs. Watson, as you requested, I've assessed our **asset quality**. In my opinion, the **percentage** of cash and cash equivalents is not high enough to provide adequate liquidity during a time of crisis. Cash reserves are a **short term** safety net against unforeseen problems. It is not **safe** for us to have them in such a small percentage. Too much of our capital is **tied up** in **hard assets**, which are difficult to liquidate on short notice.

On the same note, I suggest that we increase our percentage of securities and **cash equivalents**. Purchasing securities leads to increased liquidity, and safer overall assets. **Treasury bills** and **bonds** are always a solid investment.

Furthermore, I'd advise you to take a look at our **loan quality**. If we have a significant amount of **non-performing loans**, it's a good idea to liquidate some hard assets as soon as possible. That should provide enough liquidity to **shield** against any losses from loans.

Let me know if you would like to discuss these matters any further.

James Beery,
CPA, Branson Bank

Get ready!

❶ Before you read the passage, talk about these questions.

1 What types of assets can be accessed quickly?

2 What are the characteristics of low and high quality assets?

Reading

❷ Read the balance sheet and letter. Then, mark the following statements as true (T) or false (F).

1 __ The CPA believes the bank needs more hard assets.

2 __ The CPA recommends that the bank liquefy its government bonds.

3 __ The CPA is unsure if the bank has many non-performing loans.

Vocabulary

❸ Match the words (1-5) with the definitions (A-E).

1 __ P&E
2 __ CPA
3 __ asset quality
4 __ treasury bill
5 __ treasury bond

A a short term debt certificate

B a certified accountant

C assets including property and equipment

D the grade or degree of assets' worth

E a long term debt certificate

❹ Read the sentence pair. Choose where the words best fit the blanks.

1 **shield / tie up**

A Don't _____ assets in property, or we won't be able to access them quickly.

B _____ the bank against bad loans by checking applicants' finances.

2 **non-performing loan / loan quality**

A Banks lose money on every _____ .

B Poor _____ lowers the value of banks' assets.

3 **hard assets / cash equivalents**

A _____ can be liquidated quickly.

B _____ are difficult to turn into cash on short notice.

4 **safe / short term**

A Bonds are a _____ investment.

B Bills, unlike bonds, are _____ investments.

5 🎧 Listen and read the letter again. According to the CPA, what is the main problem with Branson Bank's asset holdings?

6 🎧 Listen to a conversation between a CPA and a senior bank officer. Choose the correct answers.

1 What is the conversation mostly about?

A completing a balance sheet

B converting hard assets into cash

C improving the bank's asset quality

D eliminating non-performing loans

2 What does the man recommend that the bank do?

A provide fewer loans

B invest in treasury bills

C hire new loan officers

D convert securities to cash

7 🎧 Listen again and complete the conversation.

Officer: I was **1** _____ _____ _____ . Let's start with the loans. What problems **2** _____ _____ _____ ?
CPA: Well, I noticed there are a few non-performing loans. If more of these come along, we're in serious trouble.
Officer: Okay. **3** _____ _____ _____ ?
CPA: I'd recommend two things. First, we need to take more time assessing **4** _____ _____ .
Officer: That's been taken care of, actually. Our loan officers are being much more thorough now.
CPA: Great. Secondly, **5** _____ _____ _____ _____ increase our cash and cash equivalents until the non-performing loans are taken care of.
Officer: **6** _____ _____ _____ _____ . That would give us plenty of cash to work with in the short term.
CPA: Precisely.
Officer: And **7** _____ _____ _____ _____ on securities?
CPA: **8** _____ _____ we need a higher percentage of them.

Speaking

8 With a partner, act out the roles below based on Task 7. Then, switch roles.

USE LANGUAGE SUCH AS:
What problems did you …?
I'd recommend …
That would give us …

Student A: You are a CPA. Talk to Student B about:
• loan quality
• cash
• securities

Student B: You are a bank officer. Talk to Student A about asset quality.

Writing

9 Use the balance sheet and letter and the conversation from Task 8 to write a recommendation about improving asset quality. Include asset types and percentages and the changes you recommend for each.

bankruptcy

bank run

suspension of convertibility

Bank Runs
Could they happen today?
by Cory Spires

The global banking system struggled recently, but don't fear. Many changes were instituted in the wake of the economic hardships of the 1930s. These have created a banking industry that is no longer susceptible to that sort of **banking crisis**.

In the past, banks operated with very little protection from the possibility of a **bank run**. A bank run occurs when a great many of a bank's customers attempt to withdraw their deposits all at once. Such hasty withdrawals can initiate a **panic**. One dramatic run can quickly close a bank's doors for good. If a bank cannot meet the demands of its depositors, it may declare **bankruptcy**. Sometimes, a bank panic will sweep across several banks, or the entire banking industry. This creates a **financial crisis**.

Fortunately, governments and financial institutions alike have implemented measures of **systemic prevention** to avoid such crises. Almost all bank customers now have accessible money in **demand deposit** accounts. Banks are now allowed temporary **suspension of convertibility**. The mere threat of this can keep a bank run from beginning. Furthermore, most commercial banks enjoy the overarching protection of **deposit insurance**. And finally, the financial industry at large is backed by the central bank as **lender of last resort**.

Get ready!

❶ **Before you read the passage, talk about these questions.**

1 What are some causes of banking crises?

2 What examples of financial crisis are there in your country's history?

Reading

❷ **Read the blog about financial crises. Then, mark the following statements as true (T) or false (F).**

1 __ The author believes the banking industry is susceptible to runs.

2 __ Bankruptcy is declared when banks cannot meet withdrawals.

3 __ Suspension of convertibility often leads to bank runs.

Vocabulary

❸ **Match the words (1-6) with the definitions (A-F).**

1 __ panic
2 __ bankruptcy
3 __ bank run

4 __ deposit insurance
5 __ demand deposit
6 __ banking crisis

A protection of accounts against bank failure

B an account from which funds are easily withdrawn

C a legal declaration of inability to pay debts

D a sudden surge of fear

E a period of unusually high risks for the banking industry

F the sudden withdrawal of funds from many accounts from a bank

4 Fill in the blanks with the correct words and phrases from the word bank.

 **BANK**

systemic prevention
lender of last resort
suspension of convertibility
financial crisis

1 The funds were unavailable due to a temporary

_____ .

2 _____ measures will avert future crises.

3 To save the institution from failure, the central bank stepped in as _____ .

4 The _____ led to several banks declaring bankruptcy.

5 🎧 Listen and read the blog again. What have governments given banks permission to do to avoid runs?

Listening

6 🎧 Listen to a conversation between a teller and a customer. Choose the correct answers.

1 What is the discussion mostly about?

A interest rate hikes

B reasons to keep an account open

C problems with the banking industry

D suspension of convertibility

2 What does the teller promise the bank will not do?

A It will not increase interest.

B It will not close his account.

C It will not suspend convertibility.

D It will not turn to the central bank.

7 🎧 Listen again and complete the conversation.

Teller: First of all, the FDIC insures all our deposits accounts, including yours.

Customer: So if the bank runs out of money, I won't lose all my savings.

Teller: Exactly. But the bank won't run out of money. We have protections against that too.

Customer: But will I have access to my money? I heard something about 1 _____ _____ _____ clauses.

Teller: We cannot suspend convertibility on demand deposit accounts. Your funds are always 2 _____ .

Customer: Even in a nationwide 3 _____ _____?

Teller: Well, yes. In that event the central bank is there as 4 _____ _____ _____ _____ .

Customer: You mean to 5 _____ _____ the entire industry.

Teller: Right. You 6 _____ _____ _____ _____ about your checking account. It's safe.

Speaking

8 With a partner, act out the roles below based on Task 7. Then, switch roles.

USE LANGUAGE SUCH AS:

But will I have access …?

You mean to …?

You don't need to worry …

Student A: You are a teller. Talk to Student B about:

● deposit insurance

● demand deposit accounts

● lender of last resort

Student B: You are a concerned bank customer. Talk to Student A about whether or not to close your account.

Writing

9 Use the blog and the conversation from Task 8 to write a newspaper article defending the safety of a bank's deposits. Include deposit insurance, demand deposit accounts, and lenders of last resort.

Get ready!

❶ Before you read the passage, talk about these questions.

1 Why are banking rules and restrictions important?

2 What laws govern banking in your country?

Reading

❷ Read the Department's mission statement. Then, choose the correct answers.

1 What is the purpose of the website?
   A to make bank recommendations to customers
   B to warn customers about banking dangers
   C to describe the purpose of an organization
   D to define regulatory guidelines and requirements

2 Which is a statement NOT made on the website?
   A Banks must show a responsible approach to market discipline to receive a license.
   B The DFO has stricter regulations than other parts of the nation.
   C A bank can lose its license if it is not in compliance with regulations.
   D The DFO believes in the idea of full reserve banking, but does not require it.

3 What can you infer about full reserve banking?
   A It is not employed by most modern banks.
   B It is a breach of regulations not to use it.
   C It has a negative impact on a bank's capital ratio.
   D It limits risk less effectively than minimum requirements.

Vocabulary

❸ Match the words (1-7) with the definitions (A-G).

1 __ breach
2 __ revoke
3 __ principle
4 __ regulatory
5 __ capital ratio
6 __ bank license
7 __ market discipline

A a basic truth or idea
B a permit that banks must have
C to invalidate something
D relationship of assets to debt
E the limit on the level of business risk
F to violate something
G relating to official rules

full reserve banking

Capital:risk

capital ratio

OCEAN CITY
Department of Financial Oversight (DFO)
M I S S I O N   S T A T E M E N T

Strong banks are the backbone of a healthy community. Here at the Department for Financial Oversight (DFO), we hope to ensure the safety of everyone's money. That is why we impose some of the most demanding banking regulations in the country.

At the DFO, we take our **regulatory** responsibilities very seriously. We expect every local bank to be in strict **compliance** with our requirements and guidelines. Banks that seriously **breach** DFO regulations will have their **bank licenses revoked**.

We also aim to help the public make informed financial decisions. Prospective depositors will find various informative resources throughout the DFO website. We recommend that banking customers consult our list of recommended banks. The list includes institutions that we believe have the most responsible approach to market discipline.

Regarding the DFO's general philosophy, we agree with the **principle** of **full reserve banking**. However, we understand that this is not a practical system in today's banking world. A successful bank can protect its depositors without having 100% of its assets in reserve. By adhering to the DFO's **minimum requirements** and carefully monitoring **capital ratio**, banks can limit financial risk. The DFO's regulations are more than sufficient to ensure the financial security of any bank's depositors.

❹ Read the sentence and choose the correct word.

1 Regulators decreased **capital ratios / minimum requirements** for local banks.

2 The bank does not have nearly enough assets for **full reserve banking / principle**.

3 The regulator checked the bank's records to ensure legal **compliance / market discipline**.

4 The bank's license was revoked after several violations of **bank licenses / regulations**.

❺ 🎧 Listen and read the website again. Why doesn't the DFO impose full reserve banking?

Listening

❻ 🎧 Listen to a conversation between a journalist and a banking regulator. Mark the following statements as true (T) or false (F).

1 ___ The journalist is writing about a bank that violated regulations.

2 ___ Capital ratios help consumers choose banks.

3 ___ The DFO increased minimum reserve requirements.

❼ 🎧 Listen again and complete the conversation.

J: Mr. Larson, I'm writing an article about financial security in today's banks. How does your organization protect bank customers?

R: The Department of Financial Oversight has many regulations that keep depositors safe. For one, we require banks to disclose 1 _____ _____ on capital ratio.

J: How does this help customers?

R: The report tells customers which banks have the strongest assets and which have the highest debt. Then customers can make 2 _____ _____ about where to store their money.

J: 3 _____ _____ the effects of the recent economic downturn? Many people are worried that even the strongest banks don't have enough money to cover their customers' funds.

R: Well, that's certainly a 4 _____ _____ . In response to the economic climate, the DFO recently increased 5 _____ _____ _____ .

J: Does that 6 _____ _____ _____ of customers' money?

R: Absolutely. If banks have more cash on hand, they will be better prepared for sudden economic changes.

J: So customers' money is more likely to be there when they need it?

R: That's right. Minimum requirements allow the bank to accommodate dramatic increases in withdrawal requests.

Speaking

❽ With a partner, act out the roles below based on Task 7. Then, switch roles.

USE LANGUAGE SUCH AS:

How does this help ...?

We have many regulations ...

In response to the ...

Student A: You are a journalist. Talk to Student B about:

● banking safety

● effect of regulations

● public concerns

Student B: You are a banking regulator. Answer Student A's questions.

Writing

❾ Use the mission statement and the conversation from Task 8 to complete the journalist's notes. Include descriptions of different regulatory practices and their effects.

regulatory

Get ready!

1 Before you read the passage, talk about these questions.

1 What is the purpose of financial regulations?
2 What are some standard financial regulations in your country?

Ferndale Savings

corporate governance

financial reporting

HOW DOES Ferndale Savings MANAGE YOUR MONEY?

At Ferndale Savings, the customer comes first. You deserve to know that your money is safe with us. That is why we provide full **disclosure** of our business practices.

Customers should expect honest and responsible **corporate governance** from a bank. Ferndale Savings complies with all agencies that **regulate** the banking industry. Our business practices continue to earn us low **credit rating requirements**. Even so, we always ensure that our funds exceed **capital requirements** and **reserve requirements**. Although the State Regulatory Committee reduced our **minimum reserve ratio** from 6% to 4%, we have maintained our high standards by remaining at 6%.

Ferndale Savings has consistently received excellent ratings from the State Regulatory Committee. We have the highest **capital adequacy** of any bank in the region, which means we will remain strong in times of emergency or economic crisis. We have also remained at the top of the Committee's list of recommended banks for six years in a row.

We are confident that Ferndale Savings is the safest place for your money. Please visit the State Regulatory Committee's website for full **financial reporting** and a comparison of Ferndale Savings to other banks.

Reading

2 Read the website and the summary. Then, fill in the blanks with the correct words from the word bank.

WORD BANK
reserves   adequacy   comply
information   recommend

Ferndale Savings ensures its customers' money is safe. They **1** _____ with all regulatory agencies. The bank has excellent credit rating requirements, but still keeps **2** _____ significantly above capital and reserve requirements. They receive consistently good ratings and have a high capital **3** _____ . The State Regulatory Committee continues to **4** _____ them year after year. Further **5** _____ is available on the Committee's website.

Vocabulary

3 Write a word that is similar in meaning to the underlined part.

1 The regulator reprimanded the bank for inadequate supply of information.
_ i _ c _ _ _ u r _

2 Poor business practices and regulations caused the bank to go out of business.
_ o _ po _ _ t e   _ _ v _ r n _ _ c e

3 The regulatory agency raised the bank's minimum asset amount.
c _ _ _ _ a l   _ _ q _ _ r e _ _ _ t

4 Bank clients need accurate presentations of business performance for financial decisions.
f _ _ a n _ _ _ l   _ e p _ _ _ i _ _

5 Banks must maintain a minimum amount of cash as directed by regulatory bodies.
r _ _ _ r _ _   _ e _ u _ _ e _ _ n _

4 Fill in the blanks with the correct words and phrases from the word bank.

capital adequacy   manages
minimum reserve ratio
regulates
credit rating requirement

1 The bankers worried that _____ was too low to accommodate the economic downturn.

2 The regulations committee _____ the practices of the local banking industry.

3 The bank's high _____ was the result of poor business decisions early on.

4 As the bank became more successful, the regulators raised the _____ to 7%.

5 The bank _____ funds for several very large accounts.

5 🎧 Listen and read the website again. What do Ferndale Savings have more of than other banks?

Listening

6 🎧 Listen to a conversation between a bank chairperson and a board member. Mark the following statements as true (T) or false (F).

1 __ The man does not know if the reserve requirement is being met.

2 __ The woman plans to personally review the reports before the meeting.

3 __ There was an error in last year's financial reporting.

7 🎧 Listen again and complete the conversation.

Board member:	The regulators want to check on our 1 _____ _____ .
Chairperson:	Well, I don't think that'll be a problem. Everything's current, isn't it?
Board member:	I'm not sure. The State Regulatory Committee raised the requirements at the beginning of the year. 2 _____ _____ _____ _____, we were getting very close to the new limit.
Chairperson:	Really? Well, get someone to 3 _____ _____ _____ before the meeting. We have to know whether we're in compliance before we 4 _____ _____ _____ . What else are they looking at?
Board member:	I'm sure they'll want to verify the accuracy of our 5 _____ _____ .
Chairperson:	Didn't they do that just recently?
Board member:	They reviewed last year's information, which was 6 _____ _____ _____ . They probably just want to see this year's.

Speaking

8 With a partner, act out the roles below based on Task 7. Then, switch roles.

USE LANGUAGE SUCH AS:

They want to check on our …

We have to know whether …

What else are they …?

Student A: You are a bank chairperson. Talk to Student B about:
- a meeting
- possible topics
- required actions

Student B: You are a board member. Talk to Student A about a meeting.

Writing

9 Use the website and the conversation from Task 8 to write the board member's report for the meeting. Include the topics that will be covered and the bank's level of compliance.

Glossary

acceptable [ADJ-U3] If something is **acceptable** it is allowed by the rule of law or social norms.

accounting fraud [N-UNCOUNT-U7] **Accounting fraud** is a misrepresentation of company funds for financial gain.

alter [V-T-U5] To **alter** is to change something.

alternative [ADJ-U1] If an investment is **alternative** it is something other than traditional investments of stocks, bonds, or real estate.

antivirus software [N-UNCOUNT-U8] **Antivirus software** is a program that is used to prevent or combat computer viruses and spyware.

apprehend [V-T-U9] To **apprehend** someone is to arrest or stop him or her.

armed [ADJ-U9] If someone is **armed**, he or she has a weapon.

arrest [V-T-U7] To **arrest** is to take someone into legal custody.

asset quality [N-UNCOUNT-U12] **Asset quality** is the probability of a loan defaulting.

bank crisis [N-COUNT-U13] A **bank crisis** is a situation in which factors in the economy cause unusually high risks for the banking industry as a whole.

bank license [N-COUNT-U14] A **bank license** is a permit that a bank must have to operate by law.

bankruptcy [N-UNCOUNT/COUNT-U13] **Bankruptcy** is a position of being legally unable to pay one's debts and usually involves a voluntary declaration of being so.

bear [V-T-U3] To **bear** something, as in a cost or a risk, is to take it upon oneself, or take responsibility for it.

bogus [ADJ-U8] If something is **bogus**, it is not real or legitimate.

books [N-COUNT-U7] **Books** are financial records.

breach [V-T-U14] To **breach** something is to break a rule or contract.

building society [N-COUNT-U2] A **building society** is a member owned financial institution that provides financial services including mortgage lending.

camera [N-COUNT-U9] A **camera** is a device that records pictures or videos.

capital requirement [N-COUNT-U15] A **capital requirement** is a minimum amount of money or assets that a bank must have available or accessible for normal business operations.

capital adequacy [N-UNCOUNT-U15] **Capital adequacy** is a measure of a bank's capital against potential losses.

capital ratio [N-COUNT-U14] A **capital ratio** is a bank's ratio of assets to debt.

card not present transaction [N-COUNT-U6] A **card not present transaction** is a purchase made by phone or on the Internet where the physical credit card isn't used.

card security code [N-COUNT-U6] The **card security code** is a group of three or four numbers on a credit card used during card not present transactions.

cash equivalents [N-COUNT-U12] **Cash equivalents** are highly liquid assets that can be quickly converted into cash.

central bank [N-COUNT-U4] A **central bank** is a public institution that controls a nation's money supply, regulates interest rates, and oversees the nation's other banking institutions.

check fraud [N-UNCOUNT/COUNT-U5] **Check fraud** is an instance where checks are used illegally to acquire money.

check kiting [N-UNCOUNT-U5] **Check kiting** is an illegal act where money is put into an account before the float period to conceal an act of fraud.

circular kiting [N-UNCOUNT-U5] **Circular kiting** is an illegal act where multiple bank accounts are used to commit fraud by transferring nonexistent sums back and forth.

club account [N-COUNT-U10] A **club account** is a savings account opened for a particular purpose that receives interest.

collateral [N-UNCOUNT-U3] **Collateral** is property pledged as security on the payment of a loan.

collection costs [N-COUNT-U11] **Collection costs** are payments which allow for debts to be collected.

combat [V-T-U5] To **combat** is to fight against something.

compete [V-I-U10] To **compete** is to challenge or try to outdo.

competition [N-UNCOUNT-U10] **Competition** is the process of attempting to succeed at something while others are attempting to be more successful.

compliance [N-UNCOUNT-U14] **Compliance** is the act of doing something that is required or requested.

comply [V-I-U9] To **comply** is to do something that someone has asked or demanded.

conservative [ADJ-U2] If an action is **conservative** it does not involve high risk. Its outcomes are predictable.

contractionary [ADJ-U4] If a monetary policy is **contractionary** it aims to lower the money supply.

copy [V-T-U6] To **copy** is to create a similar item.

corporate governance [N-UNCOUNT-U15] **Corporate governance** is the set of practices and regulations that involve the operation of a corporation such as a bank.

cost plus [N-UNCOUNT-U3] A **cost plus** contract is a business agreement in which the contractor is paid the agreed total of expenses as well as an additional profit payment.

counterfeit [ADJ-U5] If a bill is **counterfeit**, it is false, an imitation.

cover up [V-T-U7] To **cover up** is to conceal.

CPA [N-COUNT-U12] A **CPA** (Certified Public Accountant) is an accountant who is certified to audit finances.

credit card fraud [N-COUNT-U6] **Credit card fraud** is an act of stealing funds using a credit card.

credit rating requirement [N-COUNT-U15] A **credit rating requirement** is a capital requirement that is based on a bank's credit history.

credit risk [N-COUNT-U11] **Credit risk** is the risk that an investor will lose money if the borrower does not make promised payments.

debit card fraud [N-COUNT-U6] **Debit card fraud** is an act of stealing funds using a debit card.

default [N-COUNT-U11] A **default** is a case where a debtor does not make payments as legally determined by a contract.

demand [N-COUNT-U9] A **demand** is a strong or forceful statement that someone must do something.

demand deposit [N-COUNT-U13] A **demand deposit** is an amount of money placed in a bank account while remaining liquid, or readily usable.

demand draft [N-COUNT-U7] A **demand draft** is a copy of a check created by a bank.

deposit account [N-COUNT-U10] A **deposit account** is a bank account in which money can be deposited and withdrawn by the account holder.

deposit envelope [N-COUNT-U6] A **deposit envelope** is an envelope used for depositing a check or cash at an ATM.

deposit insurance [N-UNCOUNT-U13] **Deposit insurance** is a system of protecting depositors from bank failure by insuring all or a certain portion of their savings.

disclosure [N-COUNT-U15] **Disclosure** is the act of providing information.

duplication [N-COUNT-U6] **Duplication** is the act of making an exact copy.

dye pack [N-COUNT-U9] A **dye pack** is a radio-controlled device that is hidden in a stack of money and causes an explosion of colored dye when triggered. A dye pack is used to stain the money if it is stolen.

exchange rate [N-COUNT-U4] An **exchange rate** is the specified worth of one currency in terms of another.

exclude [V-T-U3] To **exclude** something is to deliberately leave it out, as in excluding usury from Islamic banking practices.

fiat money [N-UNCOUNT-U4] **Fiat money** is money that is valuable exclusively because it is recognized by a government as legal tender, and has no inherent value otherwise.

financial crisis [N-COUNT-U13] A **financial crisis** is any of a number of situations in which some financial institutions, or markets, suddenly become less valuable. These situations include banking panics, stock market crashes, and the bursting of financial bubbles.

Glossary

financial reporting [N-UNCOUNT-U15] **Financial reporting** is the presentation of a company's financial status and business performance.

financial risk [N-COUNT-U11] A **financial risk** is any risk taken with financing.

flat-fee [N-COUNT-U1] A **flat-fee** is method of payment for banking services based on a yearly percentage of the amount invested.

float time [N-UNCOUNT-U5] The **float time** is the period that exists between the time when money is withdrawn and the time when the sum is deducted from an account.

forge [V-T-U5] To **forge** is to imitate something for a fraudulent purpose.

forgery [N-COUNT-U5] **Forgery** is falsely altering or imitating something.

fraud [N-UNCOUNT-U5] **Fraud** is the use of deceit to gain money.

fraudulent [ADJ-U7] If something is **fraudulent** it was gained by dishonest means.

full reserve banking [N-UNCOUNT-U14] **Full reserve banking** is a practice in which the bank holds enough cash to cover the funds of every depositor.

getaway car [N-COUNT-U9] A **getaway car** is a vehicle used by criminals to quickly escape from the scene of a crime.

hacker [N-COUNT-U8] A **hacker** is someone who secretly accesses a secure website or system.

hard assets [N-COUNT-U12] **Hard assets** are tangible investments such as equipment, infrastructure and real estate.

hedge fund [N-COUNT-U1] A **hedge fund** is a type of private investment only available to wealthy investors, which uses certain investment strategies to limit risks and/or improve returns.

high net worth [N-UNCOUNT-U1] To have **high net worth** is to have assets that are of a monetary value greater than two million dollars.

home financing institution [N-COUNT-U2] A **home financing institution** is a lending company that specializes in making mortgage loans for the purchase of single family homes.

identity theft [N-COUNT-U6] **Identity theft** is a crime where someone uses another person's identity for financial gain.

Individual Retirement Account (IRA) [N-COUNT-U10] An **IRA** is an account where retirement funds are kept that receives tax advantages.

inflation [N-UNCOUNT-U4] **Inflation** is a rise in prices in an economy over time and subsequent lowering of the value of monetary units.

intentional [ADJ-U6] If something is **intentional** it is done with a predetermined purpose.

interest rate [N-COUNT-U4] An **interest rate** is a percentage of the principal amount of a loan, paid by the borrower to the lender.

Internet fraud [N-UNCOUNT-U8] **Internet fraud** is the act of illegally taking money or personal information from someone over the Internet while falsely promising a service in exchange.

investable assets [N-COUNT-U1] **Investable assets** are money or anything of monetary value that can be used to gain a profit.

Islam [N-UNCOUNT-U3] **Islam** is a monotheistic, text based religion, whose followers worship Allah and his prophet Mohammed, the text of which is the Qur'an, and the practice of which involves all aspects of life, including banking.

Islamic Banking [N-UNCOUNT-U3] **Islamic banking** is banking in accordance to Islamic law. It forbids the acceptance or paying of interest, and focuses on profit sharing and loss as one of its guiding principles.

joint venture [N-COUNT-U3] A **joint venture** is a business relationship in which companies or individuals come together for a specified amount of time, contributing equity to create new assets and a business entity over which participating parties share control.

leasing [V-T-U3] **Leasing** is a process by which one party is allowed use of another's assets in exchange for regular payments of a decided amount.

legal tender [N-UNCOUNT-U4] **Legal tender** is an official, legal, and legitimate currency in a given place.

legitimate [ADJ-U8] If something is **legitimate,** it is official or trustworthy.

lender of last resort [N-COUNT-U13] A **lender of last resort** is the role of a central bank when it makes short term loans to smaller banks to avoid bank runs and insolvency.

link [N-COUNT-U8] A **link** is a picture or piece of text on a website that users click on to move to another website.

liquidity risk [N-COUNT-U11] A **liquidity risk** is the risk that a security can't be traded quickly enough to make profit or prevent loss.

loan quality [N-UNCOUNT-U12] **Loan quality** is a system of grading loans based on a comparative evaluation of other outstanding loans.

loanable funds [N-COUNT-U10] **Loanable funds** are funds that are available for borrowing.

loss [N-UNCOUNT-U3] **Loss** is what occurs when returns on an investment are in the negative, or a business's total costs are greater than its profits.

manage [V-T-U15] To **manage** something is to operate or control something.

manipulate [V-T-U5] To **manipulate** is to change something for a particular purpose.

market [N-COUNT-U11] A **market** is a structure in which goods, services, and money can be exchanged.

market discipline [N-UNCOUNT-U14] **Market discipline** is the limit on the level of risk involved in a bank's business decisions, usually for the purposes of protecting its existing depositors and attracting new depositors.

market risk [N-COUNT-U11] A **market risk** is the risk that a portfolio may decrease in value because of market conditions.

minimum requirement [N-COUNT-U14] A **minimum requirement** is the minimum amount of cash or assets that a bank must keep at all times.

minimum reserve ratio [N-COUNT-U15] A **minimum reserve ratio** is the percentage of a bank's total customer deposit amount that must be kept in cash.

minimum value [N-COUNT-U1] A **minimum value** is the smallest amount of money allowed in an account to receive certain benefits, as in accrued interest, according to the account agreements.

monetary authority [N-COUNT-U4] A **monetary authority** controls the supply of a certain currency. It can be one nation's central bank or a body that controls a currency for several nations.

money market account [N-COUNT-U10] A **money market account** is a deposit account that invests in government securities and pays a variable interest rate.

money supply [N-UNCOUNT-U4] The **money supply** is the total amount of money that is available in an economy, including currency in circulation and accessible funds on record in banks.

monopoly [N-COUNT-U4] A **monopoly** is the possession of complete control over a particular product or service by one individual or company, which gives that entity the power to regulate the price and supply of that product or service.

mortgage loan [N-COUNT-U2] A **mortgage** loan is an amount of money lent to someone for the purchase of a home, the home and property being security on the loan.

mutual savings bank [N-COUNT-U2] A **mutual savings bank** is a government supported financial institution designed as a safe location for the investment of funds in mortgages, loans, stock, and bonds.

mutually held [ADJ-U2] If a financial institution is **mutually held**, its members have the power to direct the institution's financial goals.

Negotiable Order of Withdrawal (NOW) account [N-COUNT-U10] **NOW accounts** are accounts similar to checking accounts, but they earn interest.

non-performing loan [N-COUNT-U12] A **non-performing loan** is a loan that is in default.

note [N-COUNT-U9] A **note** is a brief written communication.

notice account [N-COUNT-U10] A **notice account** is an account in which the holder must give notice before withdrawal.

operational risk [N-COUNT-U11] An **operational risk** is a risk that stems from the procedures of a business strategy.

Glossary

overdraft [N-COUNT-U6] An **overdraft** is a facility to withdraw more than what's available in a checking account.

P&E [N-COUNT-U12] **P&E** (property and equipment assets) are materials purchased by a company for long term use.

panic [N-UNCOUNT-U13] **Panic** is a sudden surge of fear about something and the actions that result. A banking panic is a situation in which several banks suffer bank runs at the same time.

payable branch [N-COUNT-U7] A **payable branch** is a bank location that can cash a check.

percentage [N-COUNT-U12] A **percentage** of something is a numbered proportion out of one hundred.

pharming [N-UNCOUNT-U8] **Pharming** is the act of redirecting Internet traffic from legitimate websites to fraudulent websites.

phishing [N-UNCOUNT-U8] **Phishing** is the act of soliciting personal information over the internet by pretending to be a legitimate service or company.

portfolio [N-COUNT-U11] A **portfolio** is a collection of investments.

prevent [V-T-U11] To **prevent** is to keep something from happening.

price stability [N-UNCOUNT-U4] **Price stability** is a situation when prices in an economy change little over time.

principle [N-COUNT-U14] A **principle** is a fundamental idea or truth.

private banking [N-UNCOUNT-U1] **Private banking** is a personalized financial service provided by a bank to individuals with a large amount of money.

profit sharing [N-UNCOUNT-U3] **Profit sharing** is the economic practice wherein employees of a company receive a portion of the company's profits.

prohibit [V-T-U3] To **prohibit** something is to forbid it, or deem it not allowed.

real estate [N-UNCOUNT-U1] **Real estate** is an investment in property, including land and buildings.

redirect [V-T-U8] To **redirect** something is to alter the direction or course of something.

regulate [V-T-U15] To **regulate** something is to make official rules or requirements about something.

regulation [N-COUNT-U14] A **regulation** is an official rule or requirement.

regulatory [ADJ-U14] If something is **regulatory**, it pertains to the official rules or requirements of a particular industry.

report [V-T-U9] To **report** something is to alert police or other officials to something.

reserve bank [N-COUNT-U4] A **reserve bank** is a central bank. It controls a nation's money supply.

reserve requirement [N-COUNT-U15] A **reserve requirement** is a minimum amount of cash that a bank must have available for withdrawals from depositors.

revoke [V-T-U14] To **revoke** something is to officially cancel or invalidate something.

ring [N-COUNT-U7] A **ring** is a group of people working together for illegal purposes.

risky [ADJ-U2] If an action is **risky**, it involves high risk and unpredictability.

robbery [N-COUNT-U9] A **robbery** is the crime of stealing something by threatening someone with bodily harm.

run [N-COUNT-U13] A **run**, or run on a bank, is a situation in which a large portion of a bank's customers withdraw their deposits for fear that the bank will become unable to pay its debts.

safe [ADJ-U12] If something is **safe**, it is protected and secure.

savings and loan [N-COUNT-U2] A **savings and loan** association is a financial institution that receives savings deposits and grants mortgages and other loans.

scam [N-COUNT-U8] A **scam** is the act of making money by deceiving someone.

security [N-COUNT-U11] A **security** is a representation of financial value such as a stock or bond.

security guard [N-COUNT-U9] A **security guard** is a person whose job is to watch and protect a place from damage or harm.

security [N-UNCOUNT-U2] **Security** is a condition of reliability and safety.

Shariah [N-UNCOUNT-U3] **Shariah** is Islamic law, which determines the legality of all aspects of Islamic life.

shield [V-T-U12] To **shield** something is to protect it.

short term [ADJ-U12] If something is **short term**, it occurs during a brief period of time.

silent alarm [N-COUNT-U9] A **silent alarm** is an alarm system that alerts police or security guards to a criminal's presence without the criminal's knowledge.

sizeable [ADJ-U1] If something is **sizable** it is larger than the average amount.

skimming [N-UNCOUNT-U6] **Skimming** is illegally taking information from a credit or debit card for fraudulent purposes.

solicit [V-T-U7] To **solicit** is to request something.

spyware [N-UNCOUNT-U8] **Spyware** is a program that secretly accesses someone's computer to gather personal information and change computer or Internet settings.

SSL connection [N-COUNT-U8] An **SSL** connection is a secure Internet connection that allows information to pass between two parties without being accessed by an outside person or program.

steal [V-T-U9] To **steal** something is to take something illegally or without permission from the person who owns it.

stolen [ADJ-U6] If an object is **stolen** it was acquired by theft.

suspension of convertibility [N-UNCOUNT-U13] **Suspension of convertibility** is a bank's temporary ceasing to grant withdrawals, in order to avoid a bank run.

systemic prevention [N-UNCOUNT-U13] **Systemic prevention** is a number of different measures which aim to make bank runs less likely. These include deposit insurance, suspensions of convertibility, and central banks as lenders of last resort.

tax planning [N-UNCOUNT-U1] **Tax planning** is a financial service that involves analyzing finances for tax efficiency, and devising ways to pay a minimum amount in taxes on given assets.

threaten [V-T-U9] To **threaten** someone is to say that you will cause some harm to him or her.

thrift [N-COUNT-U2] A **thrift** is a savings and loan association.

tie up [V-PHRASAL-U12] To **tie** something **up** is to make it inaccessible.

trade [V-T-U11] To **trade** is to exchange something.

traffic [N-UNCOUNT-U8] **Traffic** is the number of people who access a particular website.

treasury bill [N-COUNT-U12] A **treasury bill** is a short term (less than one year) debt obligation issued by a government.

treasury bond [N-COUNT-U12] A **treasury bond** is a thirty year bond that is insured by the full faith and credit of a government.

unarmed [ADJ-U9] If someone is **unarmed**, he or she does not have a weapon.

uninsured deposits [N-COUNT-U7] **Uninsured deposits** are funds that are deposited into an uninsured or unlicensed bank.

usury [N-UNCOUNT-U3] **Usury** is the acceptance of a fee for lending money.

value [N-UNCOUNT-U11] **Value** is the stated worth of something.

variety [N-COUNT-U10] A **variety** is a diverse collection.

voting rights [N-COUNT-U2] **Voting rights** are the ability to vote on corporate policy decisions and board membership.

wealth management [N-UNCOUNT-U1] **Wealth management** is the overall coordination of financial services including financial planning, and investment for high net worth individuals.

yearly percentage [N-UNCOUNT-U1] **Yearly percentage** is a portion of funds invested in a given year that is decided upon as payment for banking services.

English for Specific Purposes available NOW!

www.expresspublishing.co.uk